ANTHONY FRISELL

THE

SOPRANO VOICE

A Personal Guide to
Acquiring a Superior Singing Technique

An expanded and updated edition

Branden Publishing Company
IPL series
www.brandenbooks.com
Boston

Library of Congress Cataloging-in-Publication Data

Frisell, Anthony.
  The Soprano voice : a personal guide to acquiring a superior singing technique /
Anthony Frisell. -- Expanded and updated ed.
      p. cm.
  "First English printing: Bruce Humphries, 1964."
  ISBN-13: 978-0-8283-2182-2 (pbk. : alk. paper)
  1. Singing--Instruction and study.
  2. Sopranos (Singers)--Training of.
  I. Title.

MT820.F864 2007
783.6'6143--dc22

                                        2007000585

Branden Books
Branden Publishing Company
PO Box 812094
Wellesley MA 02482

This book was written in appreciation
of the pleasure and personal fulfillment
I have experienced
during a lifetime of involvement
with the art of singing and teaching singers

CONTENTS

Are you in earnest? Seize this very minute, what you can do, or dream you can—begin it! Boldness has genius, power, and magic in it. Only engage and then the mind grows heated, Begin and then the work will be completed.

Johann Wolfgang von Goethe—
Born August 28, 1749 in Frankfurt (am main), Germany

CHAPTER ONE

The Mental Image Approach

To train the singing voice one must establish a system of vocal exercises, to accomplish that task. However, because of the physiological location of the vocal organ, these exercises *cannot* be applied in a direct manner, such as one would do to exercise the arms or legs. Therefore, all vocal exercises must be *indirectly applied,* through mental concepts. We call this method the *mental image approach.*

The beginner's mental image of her voice has such a great influence upon what she produces vocally that establishing correct mental concepts is paramount. For example, if a beginner's voice is incorrectly classified as a mezzo-soprano *(which is frequently the case with a "heavier" soprano voice,* or a soprano with *limited "head voice" development),* she will often make a conscious effort to produce vocal qualities and characteristics associated with the mezzo-soprano voice, thereby denying the true qualities and muscular needs of her own "natural" soprano voice. The first step in correcting the problem is to change the student's mental *concepts of her voice.*

By correctly applying the rules set forth in the *mental image* control theory, a formula can be had for developing the vocal organ. The formula will contain all the basic rudiments that are required, and include the *ideals of perfection* which represent the finished art of the vocal instrument. This method allows for all necessary changes for improving the voice, throughout the entire course of training. It also gives the student guiding rules, so she can compare each stage of her vocal development with the ideal.

Although it is hoped that the text is clear and explicit, the nature of signing requires that the voice student hear live performances, so that a more complete understanding of the standards of the art may be gained, by listening and experiencing. There are many who feel that most present-day singers are below par and unworthy of emulation, therefore students should seek out the best singers. Technical criticism should be directed at the way these singers use their voices and not solely at the voice itself. Singers *are not* equally endowed with great voices.

By approaching training with a *predetermined mental image*, the beginner has an outline of what is expected of her, in order to attain professional status. Singers of the past had the advantage of testing themselves in small, semi-professional opera companies, thereby smoothing out their technical problems long before submitting themselves to the judgment of audiences in the major theaters. The availability of inexpensive CD discs is another thorn in the side of the beginner; she is always being compared to the way a famous "*So-And-So* sang it on records." Very few laymen realize that the high standards of recordings are often the results of engineering skill.

Many present-day singers could well be taken to task for their attitude toward continued study of their vocal technique, once they have made their professional debuts. Most think that the few years they have studied has prepared them for any role in the repertory, and that they are free from further vocal changes and technical *"updates"*. Nothing could be less true; maintaining high vocal standards is a *lifetime study*. Even though the technique be correct, it should be understood that the *singing voice is always in a process of growing change*. To assure that the correct direction is taken, when these changes occur, the technique must possess certain fixed rules of guidance which allow for these changes and still permit the singer to continue performing.

The rules of the *vocal image control theory* must be very tangible! The highest standard attainable will completely depend upon what the singer *technically conceives of* as being correct. With continual use, some vocal experiences prove beneficial and others undesirable. By comparing the good and bad, and selecting those which the correct mental image indicates are preferable, the singer will progress from one state of vocal efficiency to a better one.

Fixed Rules: Certain fixed rules form the basis for the correct mental image

Pure vowels

The formation of pure vowels takes precedence over all other matters. The vowels are the most basic of vocal functions and the singer's most reliable methods of checking herself against bad singing habits. Distorted vowels blur the words of a musical piece and deny the singer communication with her listeners. Even if the language in which she is singing is foreign to her audience, her lack of vowel clarity soon becomes apparent in a monotony of tonal colors. From the very beginning, the singer must be determined *not* to sacrifice the purity of the vowel to attain the pitch, or tonal effect, or she will always be limited by those compromises. Each of the five Classic Italian vowels, *u (oo) i, (ee) e (eh), o (oh), and a (ah), as pronounced by native Italians*, must be mastered in their purest form throughout the entire vocal range.[1]

Control

Control cannot be over emphasized, because no matter what amount of quality or range is achieved, without control they are unreliable. Until complete control of the voice is established the singer

---

[1] The Italian pronunciation of the vowels, *u (oo) i (ee) e (eh) and a (ah)* is best for exercising the voice because it is pure, and free from diphthongs. This pronunciation should be used for all exercises in this manual.

can never pass to a state of proficiency where the technique becomes "second-natured." Mastery over the *breath-force dynamics, range, flexibility, and shading of tones* permits artistic interpretation. All are the results of control.

Musicianship

Musicianship, which is of *major importance, is often neglected or passed over too lightly.* A singer must become familiar with the rudiments of music, and acquire some ability to play a musical instrument, preferably the piano, and learn several foreign languages. Also, the nature of what is musical in vocal production should be carefully studied and cultivated. The goal of all singers should be the attainment of pure intonation, a precise sense of pitch and *legato*, genuine musical feelings, and all patterns necessary for a superior musical vocal production.

Singers must understand that, what is necessary for vocal improvement is *change,* and that this change is the result of what is technically perceived to be better. Without change the singer can only expect to perpetuate her vocal faults. In the search for vocal improvement there is always varied opinion of what is right and wrong and the student may become confused. It is always wise to pay attention to criticism, consider the sources of opinions, then permit the passing of time for testing the suggested theories. Remember that correct progress is always reflected in ease of vocal production, the overcoming of difficulties, and a positive response from your listeners.

The "Science of Voice" advocates

A matter which deserves mention, even though it is *opposed* to the simplicity of the mental image control theory, is the growing popularity with beginners to over investigate the anatomical aspects of voice production commonly referred to as the science of voice. The practice of the science of voice advocates is to directly manipulate parts of the vocal apparatus itself, in the hope of strengthening and extending the vocal range, and getting "control of the voice". For example, some of them attempt to control the actions of the tongue with an instrument called a "tongue depressor". The only correct way to control the tongue is *through special exercises*, utilizing the falsetto voice, and the i (ee) vowel. *In my latest vocal manual, The Art of Singing on the Breath Flow, all the exercises which deal with the training of the tongue and soft palate are given.*

Other advocates of the *science of voice method* depress the larynx with their thumb and forefingers. Those teachers who practice these methods of voice training attract their students by promising them a supposed faster method of voice development. The scientific speed-method always fails.

Medically speaking, medical science has made much progress in treating the victims of speech defects. However, as a method of training the singing voice, it is *useless*. Any student who submits herself to this method of training should be made aware that she is risking permanent damage of her vocal organ. Few of the great singers of the past even knew the names given of the parts of the singing instrument, much less employed them in a method of instruction. The less known in this direction, the sooner the singer will learn to depend upon and utilize *mental concepts,* which stimulate musical feelings and simplify, not complicate her task.

These aforementioned rules, which represent a correct mental image, when applied to any well used voice will only serve to confirm what is already in proper function. For the beginner, they will guide her to attaining a reliable vocal technique. For the advanced and professional singer, they serve as a reminder of the *standards to maintain.* They are, however, only a partial guide for developing a singing voice and must be extended into a more specific direction; this being the complete understanding of the *vocal registers.*

CHAPTER TWO

Identifying the Vocal Registers

To acquire a reliable vocal technique a student must have a clear concept to guide her. The functions of the *two vocal registers* serve that purpose. The vocal registers allow for definite rules of vocal control which are based on the consistent muscular patterns of the singing voice, itself. *They are very specific.* Any other means of obtaining a correct vocal production, when based solely on the *quality* and *range* of a beginner's voice, generally ends in failure.

The human voice is capable of producing many varieties of sound, of contrasting characteristics. To base the vocal technique solely on any particular sound quality is too vague a method, and because the tonal qualities used by the average beginner are generally *imitated,* and chosen to compensate for her vocal limitations, and to please her temperament. The singer who knows what the fully developed vocal registers are capable of, possesses a definite image of the ideal vocal state toward which she must strive.

Defining the Vocal Registers

A vocal register is a group of tones with harmonious qualities produced by one muscular mechanism, and it differs from another contrasting muscular mechanism, of equally harmonious qualities, timbers and strength. *To master the art of refined singing one must know the function of the two vocal registers and fully develop them, so they function together as a single unit of quality and strength throughout the entire vocal range.* There are other factors to consider, however, they are mainly matters of vowel purity/or distortion, throat constrictions, correct applications of *the breath flow,* and the irregularities of tone production which can be corrected along with the development and usage of the vocal registers themselves.

There are but two vocal registers. Within the range of the soprano voice, minor mechanical variations have been observed, and it has often been *incorrectly* theorized that there are three, or four registers. This is false, and the fallacy of the three, or four registers theory can be understood when the two registers are properly developed and united.

A permanent antagonism exists between the two vocal registers

One of the most important and generally overlooked aspects concerning the two vocal registers is that *they are antagonistic toward each other.* This *antagonism* remains in operation from the beginning phase of vocal training *(when the voice is mainly unstructured),* until the final phase of development. It is, therefore, difficult and time-consuming to subjugate the registers to a training program of muscular structuring. The accomplishment is generally known as the *"blending of the registers"*. It is this same antagonism between the two registers, which, when properly understood and used to advantage, gives the superior singing instrument its remarkable controls and qualities. These two major muscular systems, in their *"unblended"* state, strongly resist the singer's efforts to maintain control over their separate, dynamic muscular responses, denying the singer *her wish to unify all pitches of her total singing range.* Correct structuring imposes rules upon these two antagonistic muscular systems, *so they will come to function as a single muscular unit throughout the vocal range,* thereby granting the singer the necessary muscular controls over her instrument. In this way, the singing instrument functions as a *synergism.*

Before presenting additional ideas on how and what these two muscular systems contribute to the structuring process, it is necessary *to establish exactly where*, in the singer's total range of vocal tones, *the critical point of division* that separates them is *permanently* located.

Figure # 1

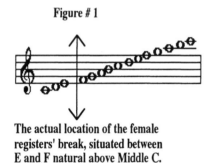

The actual location of the female registers' break, situated between E and F natural above Middle C.

Figure # 2

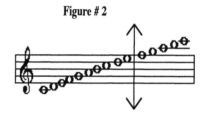

The frequently <u>mistaken</u> concept of where the female registers' break is located, between E and F natural, above C-2.

Figure #1 shows the correct position of the soprano's *Registers' Break*, situated between E♮ and F♮ above middle C. All tones below E♮ above Middle C belong to the Lower Register's muscular system, *the E♮ included.* This muscular system is generally known as the *Chest Register.* From F♮ above middle C upward, all tones belong to the *Upper Muscular System, the F♮ included.* This muscular system is generally known as the *Head Register.* The location of the Registers' Break remains in this permanently fixed position for all vocal categories, as will be explained in greater detail, later.

Many sopranos are confused or mistaken about the actual location of the registers' break, or *passaggio.* They wrongly believe their registers' break or *passaggio* to be located somewhere in the area of E2 and F2, an octave above its actual position. This mistake is understandable since the mislabeled tones *C2, C#2, D2, D#2, and E2*—an octave above middle C—often present similar problems as those presented by the tones of the actual register's break. *But the register's break area presents far more critical problems.*

Figure #2 (above), shows the frequently mistaken conception of where the registers' break is located. More about this later.

The "registers' break", and its permanent location

The point of division between the two vocal registers is most frequently referred to as the "*registers' break*". It is a natural, permanent factor of all singing voices, of all vocal categories. It has been termed a "breaking point" because when the singer with an "untrained voice" attempts to sing vocal phrases, or execute exercise scales that cross the critical break area, the muscles of the two registers, between En and Fn above middle C, frequently *"break apart"*, and refuse to cooperate in the production of satisfactory tone.

The inherent antagonism which exists between the two vocal registers can be permanently altered through selected exercises, causing them to interact in a cooperative team effort which allows for superior singing. *However, the point of division between the two registers remains forever located at its original place in the singer's vocal scale.* What changes, in order to circumvent the problems of the registers' break, is the behavior of the muscles that lie on either side of the "break point." In this new, altered, cooperative state, these transformed *"break tones"* allow the singer to sing in the "break area" with complete control of the dynamics from soft to loud and back again to soft, and to *"pronounce"* the five vowels, *u (oo), i (ee), e (eh), o (oh), and a (ah)* purely.

The vocal "passaggio"

Several tones located *below* the register's break, and several *above* it, represent an area of all singers' vocal range which presents great difficulties in singing with precise intonation, a full range of dynamics, and pure vowels. This area is frequently referred to as the vocal *"passaggio"*, an Italian word which means *passageway*. However, most female singers consider their vocal range to have "two *passaggios*", the *true passaggio*, located at the *bottom* of their range, between E♮ and F♮ natural above middle C, and a "second (*upper*) passaggio" located an octave *above* the true registers' break. The specific tones of the reported *upper break* are E2 and F2 above C2.

It is critical for all sopranos to structure the "*true (lower) passaggio*" tones to a state of perfection in order to achieve a superior standard of vocal production, and a full range, since the tones that are located between the "lower break" and "upper break"—F♮ to B♮ above middle C—can never be correctly structured, unless the lower *"true break"* has been correctly structured. It takes *many years* of hard work to bring the "lower break's" *passaggio* tones to a state of perfection. Throughout this manual many references will be made to the problems that the *passaggio* presents to all sopranos, and the various exercises to overcome them.

Some basic characteristics and terms that are often applied to the two vocal registers

The Lower Register

Both vocal registers contribute important muscular actions and tonal qualities to the singing instrument. These actions provoke descriptions based upon subjective impressions. The vocal sounds of the lower register's range of tones *(the "chest voice")*, are often referred to as *"resonance"* or *"vocal solidity"*. This register contributes the basic power factor (*"vocal projection" in the theater*), to the singing instrument. Some familiar *terms that attempt to describe the variety of tonal qualities contributed by the lower register are: "ring", "bite", "core", "solidity", and "resonance"*. The term "resonance" is *incorrectly* applied, as it correctly describes the *resounding* of the *vibrato action* of the vocal cords, within a given resonance chamber. The vocal sounds of singing are the result of the vibrating action of the vocal cords set into a vibratory motion by "breath pressure" that is being applied to them, which in turn produces the intensification or prolongation of sound, produced by sympathetic vibrations, within one of the resonance cavities of the singing voice. The vibrato action of the vocal cords is a correct and desired function of the vocal instrument.

The Upper Register

The vocal sounds of the upper register's range of tones *(the "head voice")* or the *"falsetto"* register are most often referred to as *"sweet"* or *"ethereal"*, and its muscular actions contribute *beauty of vocal tone, flexibility of control, and vocal shading*. Some of the terms applied to its range of tonal qualities are: *"the clear voice", "the child's voice", "tonal freshness", "purity of tone", "overtone"*, the *"thin register"*, and the *"whistle voice"*.

Paradoxically, one set of the *five basic vowels* can be produced in the *lower register*, maintaining the sounds and muscular characteristics indigenous to that register, while *another set of the five vowels* can be produced in the *upper register* maintaining the sounds and muscular characteristics indigenous to that register. *Yet*, when the singer attempts to combine the basic sounds and muscular actions of the lower register's vowels with those of the upper register's vowels, on any given tone or groups of tones, it is impossible to achieve a match or "blend" of the registers' sounds and muscular actions. Only when the two registers have been completely restructured will they allow for their mutual exchange of qualities and muscular actions to occur.

This refusal, by the registers, to exchange their basic muscular actions and tonal qualities is a tangible and graphic demonstration of the undeniable division that exists between these two major muscular systems. This conflict is acknowledged by the international community of vocal musicologists. Many technique books have been written that discuss the subject of the vocal registers, the mystifying registers' break that separates them, and the difficulty the registers' break presents when the singer executes an extended vocal scale, either ascending or descending through the registers' break area, with the intention of unifying all the tonal qualities and muscular actions of each and every tone, throughout the vocal scale. It has seldom been stated, however, that the problems caused by the registers' break are the same factors which, when understood, can be used advantageously, as the tools for correctly structuring a superior vocal instrument. The purpose of this manual is to explain and clarify the antagonisms of the two registers, toward each other, and to outline the precise methods of using them in a reliable and consistent vocal structuring program.

When a soprano attempts to sing phrases that ascend from the bottom of her range toward the *middle range* area, using a reasonably strong volume, and the a *(ah) vowel,* unless the *true, "lower" registers' break area* has been correctly structured, she is denied the attainment of correctly-functioning, beautiful tones in that area, and she is forced to compromise their quality, volume, and control. These compromises manifests themselves as *impure vowels,* and *harsh, unmusical tones.* This unsatisfactory vocal condition may be referred to as a state of *"antagonistic vocal registers",* meaning the singer has not managed to circumvent the basic antagonism that exists between the two registers. The singer with this vocal condition usually possesses a voice with strong, thick lower and middle range tones, a few faulty, barely accessible tones in the registers' break area, and, above the registers' break area, forced, unmusical tones that are *"weak", "hollow", "uncoordinated", and "unmatched"* in tonal quality to the lower and upper areas of her range.

This singer's upper tones are *disadvantageously dominated* by the muscular controls of the *chest voice,* and are in need of the help of the head voice muscles. But correcting this matter *is not* simply a matter of totally eliminating the participation of the chest voice muscles *(as is presently, generally believed),* since *the chest voice's muscles play an important role in the restructuring of both the true registers' break area,* and the tones that are located just above it, plus the soprano's so-called *"upper register break".* In order to overcome the unavoidable antagonism that exists between the two registers they *must be muscularly blended,* through a long and slow process of *"restructuring",* so that they function as one, both in action and tonal quality, throughout the singer's complete range.

Because there exist so many conflicting muscular actions, tonal varieties, and variations of physical sensations, and confusing sounds between these two major muscular systems, which cause them to *permanently react antagonistically toward each other, a controversial question always arises* as to what, *precisely,* about these two registers *is* "accurate", where superior singing is concerned. Therefore, we must establish a ruling principle as a foundation for further development.

A ruling principle

The conflicting muscular responses that occur, between the two vocal registers, when attempting to produce pure, superior vocal tone, *represent the natural responses to the energy of the motor force (breath tension) being applied to the muscles of both registers, in order to achieve that goal.* We can begin to understand the antagonistic nature of the two muscular systems by thinking of their basic response to each other as *a form of tug-of-war,* each register struggling for dominance over the other. The *lower register,* however, has many advantages over the weaker upper register. It is generally the stronger of the two registers, at the onset of vocal training.

There are several factors that contribute to the dominance of the lower register, over the upper register:

1. The muscle groups that produce the lower register's complete range of tones *(though they be fewer than the soprano's upper register's tones),* are inherently larger, and occupy a larger physiological "space *(windpipe and neck),* than do the muscle groups that produce the upper register's range of tones *(physiologically located in the mouth-pharynx, and head cavities).* Applying this principle to soprano voices is complex, since their vocal range, when fully developed, must contains more *"head tones"* than *"chest tones".* Yet, those few *"chest tones"* tones that remain are critically important to the proper function of the voice, since without them the entire range would *"closed down" (more about this in detail, later).*

2. Most training programs apply their basic exercises to the bottom of the singer's vocal range *(through ascending scales),* where the lower register is most powerful. *This gives the lower register yet another advantage* over *the inherently weaker upper registe*r in winning the tug-of-war between the two registers.

3. Most singers are often volume-conscious, impatiently seeking the *quick* attainment of *"resonant, powerful, professional-sounding tones".* They fail to consider the developmental attributes of *the softer, detached falsetto's muscular controls of the upper register,* especially with the tones located just above the *Lower Registers' break F♮* above middle C—which are more subtle, and can only be invoked and strengthened by starting off with softer tonal dynamics. These falsetto *tones* take much longer to develop. And even longer to reveal their true tonal qualities and muscular strength *than* do the *readily-available chest tones.* The valuable, long-range benefits derived from cultivating the softer and subtler *(but in no way weaker, when properly developed),* muscular controls of the upper register's softer falsetto tones are frequently neglected by the *"volume-conscious singer".* This is because, in their earlier phase of development, the falsetto muscles produce only *"thin", "non-resonant"* tonal qualities that are easily *misunderstood* as being unrelated to the advanced, full-volume, *"legitimate"* performing voice.

The true worth of the first, falsetto starter-tones that are produced by the average beginner are *misleading.* It should be noted that, at the beginning of training, correctly interpreting the true value of these tones *(as they progress in strength and yield benefits to the singer),* and rendering judgments, regarding quality of tone, *should be reserved for expert ears.* Despite the inherent dominance of the lower register, the singer or voice teacher, armed with accurate, specialized knowledge, can play a major role in deciding which of the two vocal registers will eventually emerge as the dominant register.

Resolving the conflict between the two vocal registers can be accomplished, in part, by favoring the upper register. In the past, training programs utilized specialized exercises that gave preference to the *falsetto tones' growth and development,* with the intention of *it* dominate most of the muscular controls of the singer's complete range of tones. This dominance of the falsetto voice of the singer's complete range of tones, in *no way excludes the brilliance and power of the lower (chest) register, but rather assures that it is applied safely.* The *chest voice,* when operating *without* the *collaboration of the upper register,* can be damaging to the singing voice. *During the early period of training,* the muscular activities of the *chest register* must be relegated to a *temporarily* passive and subordinate role.

Many singers and teachers avoid a program of *"falsetto"* training because the falsetto sounds produced during the early building process are *unfamiliar,* when compared to the sounds of the chest voice *(even when they are incorrect).* To most individuals, the falsetto's sounds appear remote and confusing. This occurs because these various, *"unusual sounds"* of the *developing* falsetto voice, and the positive results they can exert upon the developing singing voice, *have not been heard* in most training studios for many decades, *and have not,* therefore, been passed down to present-day vocal teachers. This has set in motion an unfortunate, downward spiral in the quality of singing.

At the beginning of this *head voice training program,* the singer is generally dealing with underdeveloped muscular conditions, *in both the upper and lower registers,* in which state they are incapable of producing the beautiful, highly-controlled tones of the advanced vocal state. This advanced vocal state can only be attained over a long period of time, and only through technical knowledge and discipline. One of the most blatant faults of contemporary training occurs when teachers fail to make allowances for the *"raw", "crude",* almost *uncontrollable* vocal sounds that most beginners must produce, during the early phases of training. Most teachers instead attempt to quickly draw from their students *"polished", "beautiful", "solid"* and highly-controlled vocal sounds which can only be produced by advanced professionals. For an untrained voice to progress from the crude vocal sounds of an amateur to the beautiful and highly-controlled vocal sounds of a professional is a matter of correct muscular development of the vocal instrument, which takes a great deal of time and correct knowledge to accomplish. It is not a matter of the singer comprehending the *"esthetics, beauty and subtleties of refined singing"* which some teachers wrongly assume, or imitating a famous artist of the day.

Professional singers, too, are guilty of hindering beginners, in their failure to give testimonies of their earlier, *less ideal stages* of vocal development, when they *could not* produce controlled beautiful tones. In this way, they must be considered *silent partners* in the conspiracy of ruinous vocal training methods being practiced today, which do not allow the beginning singer her individual rate of vocal development.

With an untrained voice, *the muscular condition of her vocal registers is dysfunctionally divided,* a negative state wherein the two registers *do not* function harmoniously with each other. In this state, the singer often possesses a limited vocal range, unclear, "muddy", vowels, muscular conflicts and tonal inconsistencies. The lower register, in this state, produces sounds that are *thick and unmusical*. When the soprano ascends a vocal range, using tones of the lower register, the scale eventually reaches the point of encounter with the weaker, thinner tones of the upper register system *(as these tones invariably exist, prior to proper development, and register blending)*, and the attempted, ascending scale is frequently unsuccessful.

Most sopranos, in an understandable attempt to extend the *"solidity factor"* of their lower range upward, frequently force the action of the *chest voice* past the registers' break, situated between E♮ and F♮ above middle C. This immediately halts the process of correct structuring, and in some cases, causes permanent damage. *The first major step in the long process of properly structuring the singing voice is for the singer to begin performing a series of exercises that will permanently reduce the undesirable bulk and thickness of the lower register*. This does not *"discard"* the chest voice permanently, but merely *"holds its power in check"* until the proper time to again call upon its important muscular contributions, and tonal qualities.

Generally, with Soprano voices, the appropriate *"strong and resonant"* sounds of the *vibrato action* of the vocal cords are not readily understood, nor easily evoked, because they are produced by the *chest register*, which is usually completely neglected by most sopranos, attempting to train their voices. The essential difficulty, for the soprano voice, is to transport the strong, vibrant sounds of the vibrato action *(chest voice)* upward and into the tones located just above the registers' break. These particular tones, in their initial, underdeveloped state, are *weak, thin, hollow and breathy*, and seem unrelated in quality and muscular action to those produced by the lower *(chest)* register. Only with advanced development will the soprano be able to properly transport the power of the chest voice upward, through the lower *passaggio* into the thinner region of head voice's lower tract, which is located just above the register's break, at F♮ above middle C, then further upward in her range. Some important advice, about the *"breathiness"* of the above mentions tones, situated just above the registers' break—*make no attempt to stop what you incorrectly termed "wasted, escaping air" with these tones! Later on, you'll need that precious air, in order to mix it with the solidity factors of the chest voice.*

During the long, structuring process, the task for all sopranos is to strengthen these undeveloped, upper register falsetto tones *(by applying the messa di voce exercise)*, until they have adopted the resonant, vibrant quality of the lower register, without losing the beauty and dominant muscular control of the upper register. Then, *they* will *"invite"* the addition of the *chest voice power* to join them, *completely on their own. Avoidance of this critical issue is a guarantee for vocal failure, usually sooner than later.*

The process of developing the muscular controls of the underdeveloped falsetto tones is slow and difficult to achieve. But, when successfully accomplished, these controls give the singer's listeners the impression that all tones of her vocal range are produced with a single muscular system. For the singer, it accomplishes the much admired *"seamless vocal scale"* throughout her complete range. But, the reality of this seamless vocal scale is quite different from the perception of *the singer's listeners*. They hear and believe that all the tones of the singer's range are produced with a single muscular system, when in truth, the singer employs separate teams of muscular controls throughout her entire range, over which she has become mistress, during a long and tedious training period.

The master-singer develops a method of muscular controls which allows her to transfer her singing of certain notes from one "team" to the next team, with a smooth *legato*, superior tone, and pure vowels. The selection of a particular team of muscles to handle a specific vocal maneuver, is relative to the area of vocal range which the musical piece demands. The most important factor is to accomplish the transfer of muscular control from one muscular team to the next in such a smooth, imperceptible manner, so that her listeners can't hear it being accomplished. More information about this will be presented later on, plus the discrepancies between what the listener hears and what the singer is "actually doing". The subject has been touched upon at this early part of the manual to start the reader thinking about the complexities of *"playing"* the singing instrument. Singing is too often thought of in passive terms, which suggests that after the voice has been completely development, it could "sing itself".

The metamorphoses of the two vocal registers

One of the main reasons that most vocal training methods fail to develop superior vocal instruments, for hopeful students is because, the singer does not understand the nature of the various muscles of the registers and attempts to use them in their undeveloped state. Frequently, the student is assigned a *series of rote, meaningless ascending scales* that will never enable her to meet the demands of professional singing. Seldom is it considered that the vocal instrument must be calculatingly structured. The vocal instrument is not completely nor perfectly assembled, waiting for the student to merely learn how to play it. On the contrary, all superior voices are *"created"* by muscular structuring, achieved by transforming the undeveloped muscles of the two vocal registers *(from whatever starting condition in which they initially present themselves),* to a *"new", "improved"* state of structural existence, one that meets the physical challenges of singing all sorts of demanding vocal literature.

This vocal transformation is accomplished by executing a series of selected exercises that favor the development of the upper register, so that it becomes the dominant muscular system, over the chest voice. These exercises are performed in ways that prepare the singer for the similar ways that she will eventually use them, when her *"vocal organs"* are fully developed, and while actually singing. Most present-day vocal exercises are *"anti"* singing and throw the voice "out of order." Most modern-day singers who accomplish a quality singing voice eventually avoid exercises, and attempt to sing without vocalizing, and hope for the best.

When submitting to a training program that temporarily favors the upper register, what gradually becomes evident to the student is that, the muscles controlling the *upper register* grow in strength, *first* within their original boundaries, *and later they* become stronger and capable of being transported outside those boundaries, downward in the vocal range, *and can overlap all the tones of the chest register.* Once this has been accomplished, the developed, restructured upper register's muscular controls dominate all the tones of the singer's complete range. *In that state, they all function within a singular, unifying arc of the head voice's muscular controls.* However, *they are still not sufficiently structured,* for superior singing. *This is so because, the upper register's controls are not sufficient in-and-of-themselves to accomplish all the vocal tasks of the singing instrument, nor can they alone grant beauty and control of all the tones of the complete range. They require the full, complimentary participation of the lower register's muscles to do so.*

This point must be well noted, since many sopranos who embark upon a *"head voice"* voice training program feel that, once their upper register has advanced and they can sing rather well *(for the time being, of course),* they are free from all involvement with the *"thick"* and *"cumbersome"* chest voice. Nothing could be further from the truth, because, when the controls of the *chest voice* are denied, the result is always unattractive, uncontrolled, unprofessional singing, and eventually a total vocal collapse.

During the upper register's transformation from subordinance, to a state of dominance over the chest voice, the process automatically imposes a corresponding transformation on all the tones of the lower register. In proportion to the ongoing development of all upper register tones, the chest voice's tones begin shrinking, reducing their "weight" and "thickness," and they gradually subjugate themselves to the controls of developing falsetto, which the singer must continuously transport downward from the top range, and make these controls overlap the complete bottom range, thereby asserting their positive influences upon the *bottom range,* until all its tones willingly participate with the head voice, in a "team effort". This first, major phase of the correct structuring process is not unusual, since most professional sopranos have instinctually already brought the two vocal registers to this stage. However, what is still missing is clear and specific knowledge of how to bring back into play the muscular controls of transformed and subjugated chest voice, which were temporarily set aside.

This is gradually accomplished by continuously saturating the tones of the registers' break with ample amount of the breath flow, using the *u (oo), o (oh), or AW vowels,* until the registers' break tone allow the *"power"* factor of the lower register to pass upward in the range beyond the registers'' break *(situated between E♮ and F♮ above middle C), then further upward to the Top Range.* As a result, the *vibrato action* of the chest voice then flows, on the energized breath stream, freely upward from the *Bottom Range,* past the registers' break area, and into the tones of the *Top Range,* granting the singer's voice the long-time, missing, *"ring", "resonance" and "projecting power" factors* to all their tops tones, as well as the rest of their range. This is often called a state of *"harmonic registers".* With *harmonic registers,* all the tones of the singer's lower range, freed from the chest voice's negative bulk and weight, and transformed into "buoyant, breath-flow tones", the singer is able to *"thread"* the *power factor* of the lower register into each and every tone of her complete range.

Meanwhile, a related phenomenon occurs with all the tones of the *Top Range*. They begin to extend beyond their original borders, at both their upper and lower ends. When this advanced development is reached, the now dominant muscular contours *(or" walls")*, of the *upper register channel* possess sufficient strength to hold the *"raw"* action of the lower register's tones *"in check"*, so that their original bulk is blocked and transformed, then *"squeezed into a thinner form"* in which they can easily be joined to the flexible contours of head voice's entire range. This in possible because, unlike the rigidity of the chest voice's *"walls"*, the head voice's *"walls"* are *highly malleable*. With the two registers joined together, it this new compress, *"gathered"* form, both registers readily adapt to and synergistically collaborate with each other, to produce beautiful, highly-controllable vocal tones.

The lower register's tones begin to sound *"lighter"* in weight and feel, to the singer, *"airy and buoyant"*. And, they actually are, due to the fact that the *breath flow,* which originates in the *Top Range,* has been transferred downward and infused into all the tones below it. In time, they become *"puffy"* and *"vibrant"* to the singer. At the same time, all the developing tones of the *upper register* begin to take on *a more solid* sound that is *"like"* the sounds of the lower register.

All these changes are natural, when structuring practices gives the upper register preferred treatment. All these *"mixed sounds"* and transformed muscular responses, precede the arrival of the *mezzo-falso, or mixed voice (see p. 112).* (see p. 112) The *mixed voice* is a mechanism of muscular control that results when the two registers begin to approach total muscular harmony with each other. Teachers of the *Bel Canto* period termed these sounds the voce *di finta,* or *"feigned voice",* which means that the quality and sound of the advanced developed falsetto *"feigns"* a likeness to, or pretends to be muscularly the same as the chest voice.

When this *mixed voice* mechanism finally appears, it allows the singer to initiate a soft tone within the upper register's domain *(and eventually, in all other areas of the range),* that is still falsetto-sounding, but it also possesses a solid brilliance, similar to the chest voice. The *mixed voice* allows the singer to press together both registers' muscular actions, for the duration of a chosen tone, by continuously applying appropriate amounts of breath pressure to it. When the two registers are tightly *"clamped"* together in this manner, the singer can gradually add to any soft *"mixed tone"* the full power, and the *"bright"* quality of *the chest voice*, and then withdraw it, at will. Often, this skill takes years to master, with certain pitches.

The development of the mezzo-*falso or "mixed voice"* mechanism is a requirement for all singers. The *mixed voice* must be made to exist and operate throughout the complete range, so that passing back and forth, from one register's muscular control, to the other registers controls, on the same tone, subjugates both registers to a *"team effort",* completely eliminating the antagonism which formerly existed between the two registers.

If the *mezzo-falso* is referred to, at all, in present-day training procedures, it is generally called the *"mixed voice",* a term adapted from the French term *voix mixte. However,* the term *"mixed voice",* is inappropriately used. This is because "mixed" implies that the separateness of the two registers becomes blended into one, single, third unit, thereby becoming something new and different. This is *not* what actually takes place. The muscular actions of both register never merge or "mix" into a new, single unit. They remain separate entities which function together as a "team". Their individual muscular controls lineup vertically, "side-by-side, and work together in the production of all superior tones, while each muscular controls retains its inherent individuality, and can be completely separated from the other (s). *(see pgs. 134-124—"The Three Vocal Layers).*

At the point where the two advanced developed registers make a harmonious contact with each other and can be clamped together by the singer, there comes to exist a neutral point of their contact with each other, that has been created through the perfection of the *messa di voce (p. 67).* The *messa di voce* is an important exercise which starts by the singer establishing a tone in the *"detached falsetto"* mechanism *("detached" from all chest voice power),* and slowly increasing its volume until the full power of the chest voice is gradually added to the starter-tone. This can only be accomplished when the inherent bulk of the chest voice has been restructured to a *minimal* throat-space, and the *Upper Register's* tones have been brought to their *maximum* strength. This creates a physiological, harmonious point of contact between the *chest and head voice registers* wherein *neither's muscular controls dominate the other register.* Stated another way, when they are able to make contact with each other at a specific point *(in the upper posterior area of the throat),* where the negative and uncooperative aspects of both registers have been neutralized, by the successful *messa di voce* exercise.

This *neutral point of encounter* is controlled by the singer, by first understanding how the muscular *force and volume* of both registers' throat-spaces can be proportionately reduced to their minimum, then *"pinched"* or *"clamped"* together , ready for the singer to instigate the vocal maneuver of the moment, whether to perform a *fortissimo* or *piano* tone. The *mezzo-falso* mechanism permits the singer selectivity of the size of the throat-space of a selected tone, plus a full range of potential dynamics, from soft to loud, then back to soft again.

The *mezzo-falso* mechanism allows the singer the ability to regulate the volume of a selected tone without either register's muscular controls challenging the muscular controls of the other register, and without either register's muscular controls being negated, or abandoned nor compromised.

It is only when the both registers' volume can be greatly reduced and *"suspended"* at a neutral point of dynamic contact with each other, that the singer can begin to execute a true *pianissimo.* A true *pianissimo* should display the qualities of *both* registers, but with the dynamic level of each register reduced to its softest. A *"faked" pianissimo* utilizes the contributions of upper register *almost exclusively (without sufficient chest voice participation),* and results in a *"wooly"* tone, without core substance, and no potential for *"projection".* This kind of *"vocal forgery"* is in common usage among professional singers today.

The basic tools of the "breath force" used for all vocal exercises

In order for the singer to properly develop the muscles of her singing instrument, it is necessary for those muscles to be stressed. This is done by progressively increasing the amount of breath force that is applied to a selected tone, until the desired developmental result is achieved. The process is not unlike *progressive weight training,* practiced by *"body builders"*. The tools that permit the application of the various intensity levels of the breath force to any selected tone (s), are:

1. Breath tension *(motor force).*

2. Variations of breath tension *dynamics—p, pp, ppp—f, ff, fff, for example*

3. The application of the five classic Italian vocal vowels, each of which adjusts the flow of the breath flow, in its own, individual manner.

1. Breath tension (motor force)

The first basic tool used to exercise the muscles of the singing voice is *breath tension,* which creates the *motor force* necessary to produce a tone and to stress it. *Breath tension* is achieved by inhaling a *full amount of air,* compressing it within the lungs, then directing it, *(in the form of an intensified stream),* against the vocal cords. There are two cycles in the breathing process:

1. Intake: *inhalation* — *2.* Output: *exhalation*

Inhalation must be executed very slowly. The muscles involved with inhalation, located below the singer's lowest ribs, are to be activated first, while the muscles above the lowest ribs *(circling all around the waist),* are to be kept *as passive as possible.* This process is often referred to as *"low breathing"*, and it allows the fullest possible amount of air to be inspired into the lungs. Even so, the amount of air *(breath tension),* to be used by the singer varies, depending on the pitch and/or phrase, presently being sung.

At the end of the *intake cycle,* when the lungs are completely filled with air, by withholding it from leaving the lungs *"breath tension" is created.* While holding back the air, there occurs a critical moment of breath suspension, granting the singer the potential for utilizing this breath force for the production of vocal tone. This is accomplished by quickly transferring the *"held-in breath"* over to the *"outgoing-cycle"* of exhalation. The singer must direct the *breath stream* directly against her vocal cords, which then assume the form of a narrow, intense stream of compressed air. The slender, intense breath but powerful stream of breath quickly passes through the vocal cords, then upward, through the wind pipe. The singer must then direct the *breath stream* into an appropriate *resonance cavity,* either into the *mouth-pharynx,* or into the cavities of the *sinuses* or cavities of the *skull.*

During the above maneuvers, the vocal cords react to this stream of intensified air *(the prolongation of which is regulated by the diaphragm and other various muscles of the breathing apparatus),* by elastically yielding to it, in a series of *rapid openings and closings.* This causes a slight rise and fall in the pitch of the selected tone, as the vocal cords yield to the stream of breath pressure being exerted against them. This response of the vocal cords is known as *vibrato,* and it is essential for correct singing. Reacting in conjunction with, and in response to the application of the breath force directed to the vocal cords, the *upper register's muscles (which tend to pull upward, and the chest voice's muscles which tend to pull downward),* are simultaneously brought into play. Acting as a "team", these "upward and downward pulling muscles" hold the entire vocal mechanism taut, while also acting as counter-resistants to the energy of the breath tension being directed at the vocal cords.

The *vibrato* and the co-participation of the *upper* and *lower* register muscles cannot be directly controlled. Skillfully utilizing their functions is dependent upon a correct application of breath tension to the muscles of both registers, through various throat adjustments, which can only be evoked and set into motion through proper mental concepts and images.

The singing tone is produced by allowing the vibrations of the vocal cords to travel on "the energized breath stream," toward a selected pitch, located within a particular resonance cavity. One of the most misleading concepts told to students is to accomplish an *"effortless, tone that floats".* This implies that the singer is free from any *work load,* in producing basic tone. The superior tone is *never free from a work load,* because it is produced by the energy of the compressed air, withheld within the lungs, which the singer skillfully *"feeds"* to the vocal cords. As the singe ascends her vocal range to higher pitches, the amount of pressure, *directed against the cords,* must be increased proportionately, and an equally increased amount of energy is demanded of the singer. Conversely, when the singer descends her range from a higher pitch to a lower one, this breath pressure is gradually *withheld and reduced* by the singer. *But it is never entirely eliminated,* for there must always remain some amount of breath pressure being withheld within the lungs and directed against the vocal cords, or they will stop vibrating. This breath pressure, contained within the lungs, is necessary to *"hold"* or *"clamp"* the two registers together in order to produce the pitch and vowel being presently sung, while the singer *holds her throat appropriately open,* so that they serve as a counter-resisting force to the breath pressure, being directed toward the pitch being presently sung.

The least efficient way of breathing, where singing is concerned, is the *shallow intercostal method.* Instead of the diaphragm being free to expand downward and outward *(in the form of a "circle" that surrounds the waistline, and moving outward, in all directions, away from the body)*, to allow the fullest inhalation, it is *incorrectly* drawn inward then inverted upward, and the entire chest cavity is raised. This incorrect method allows for only *a partial inhalation of breath* and interferes with the attainment of *a full breath* which is so critical to creating the required breath pressure that must act as a motor force, for the production of the tone. Singers who employ this incorrect method of breathing *(women, more frequently than men),* tend to gulp for air between phrases, raising their upper ribs and clavicles. This method produces undesirable tensions with muscles that should remain passive, and it forbids thoracic expansion and the freedom of the diaphragm.

Correct breathing depends on *coordinating the muscular staying power of the exhalation*. When breathing is correctly executed, there is no deficiency of breath at the end of a phrase, but rather some excess, *which must be fully expelled, before taking a new breath.*

In order for the *breathing system* to grow progressively stronger, to meet the demands of the singing instrument, the "breathing muscles" must be developed to their fullest. However, they *can not* be strengthened in an independent manner, separate from the production of tone. Their strengthening is conditioned upon, and regulated by the strengthening of the muscles of both the upper and lower registers. As the muscular controls of the registers grow in strength, particularly the upper register, so does the singer's capacity for superior breathing.

To produce the wide range of vocal pitches contained in a musical piece, varying amounts of compressed air are required; *a lesser or moderate amount of breath tension is required for low and medium pitches,* and a greater amount *for the higher pitches.* While vocal tone is being sung, the vocal cords allow the breath to escape through the glottis in short, *"puffy"* blasts, which slowly and simultaneously dissipate the compressed air that is being "held back" within the lungs. To maintain control of the prolongation of a tone, this gradual dissipation of breath tension must be regulated by the muscles of the two vocal registers, assisted by the diaphragm, which resists the dissipation of the breath tension by acting as counter-resistants. Reacting from polarity positions *(from throat positions, above and below the vocal cords),* the two registers act together in a drawstring manner. While the breath pressure exerted against the vocal cords tends to move the entire vocal apparatus *"forward"*, the counter-resistance of the two vocal registers tends to move it *"backward".* While singing, despite the vocal apparatus' need for maintaining *"flexibility of movement"* the two registers' counter forces, acting in unison with each other, maintain a constant, fixed position of the vocal apparatus, relative to the production of the tone being presently sung.

The potential growth of the breathing system is conditional upon how long the singer can maintain the compressed air in the lungs, while gradually *"feeding"* it to the vocal cores, and producing a superior sustained tone, that rides on the energized breath stream. The longer the duration of a tone or phrase *(particularly where the higher pitches are concerned),* the greater the stress which the muscles of the breathing system must sustain, therefore, the greater is the breathing system's development, when that stress can be successfully tolerated and satisfied. However, the muscles of the breathing system cannot accommodate these increases of stress *unless* the muscles of the two registers are capable of producing equal amounts of counter-resistance to the breath force.

2. The three methods of applying breath tension dynamics to the singing instrument

It is imperative for the singer to develop an ability to apply varying levels of breath tension to the muscles of a selected tone, in order to develop its strength and beauty. This *breath tension* is available to her at various dynamics of loudness and/or or softness, and from minimum to maximum, and they can be incrementally applied to the selected tone. The selected tone's tolerance for progressively increased amounts of breath tension also determines the pace and rate of development, of the singer's breathing skills. The options for applying dynamic variation of the breath stream tension, as outlined by the *Bel Canto School* of vocal training, are three:

Figure 1, the *messa di voce:* a tone is started *pp* and gradually increased to a *ff.*

Figure   1

The *messa di voce*

Figure 2, the *esclamazio viva:* a tone is started with *ff* intensity, gradually reduced to *p* intensity, then returned to its original intensity.

Figure   2

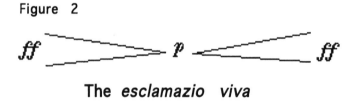

The *esclamazio   viva*

Figure 3, the *esclamazio languida:* a tone is started with *p* intensity, gradually increased to *f* intensity, reduced again to *p ,* and finally increased to *ff* intensity.

Figure   3

The *esclamazio languida*

The *messa di voce,* the *esclamazio viva,* and the *esclamazio languida* were the three most important *breath-tension* applications applied, during the *Bel Canto* era. For practical reasons, based on the needs of various voices during critical stages of their development, I have created a new group of exercises based upon these same three *bel canto* classic applications, which update their method of application to accommodate contemporary vocal repertory.

3. The five vocal vowels

To execute the various exercises necessary for developing the singing instrument, the singer must have a complete understanding of the muscular functions of the five basic Italian vowels—*u (oo), i (ee), e (eh), o (oh), and a (ah)—as they are pronounced by native Italians*. Each individual vowel commands movements of the *tongue, lips and cheeks,* and various adjustments of the posterior areas of the throat, the both vocal registers, as well as the vocal cords. *The only way the singer has of translating vocal muscularity into vocal tone is via the assistance of the five classic Italian vowels, operating in conjunction with the breath flow.*

The Mechanical functions of the five singing vowels: u (oo), i (ee), e (eh), o (oh), and a (ah)

With every musical instrument, other than the singing voice, the performer can touch the instrument directly with his hands, in order to exercise or play it. The singer's instrument, on the other hand, is inaccessible, and can only be evoked and controlled through the use of mental concepts and images that relate to the function of the five basic vowels, which serve to set the physical mechanism *(the muscles),* into motion.

Vocal repertory involves a marriage of text and musical tones, and within any given syllable of a particular word there is *a dominating vowel* that will correctly activate pure tone and set the throat into a specific *(vowel)* throat position. *Each pure vowel sound is created by its own individual muscular functions, which must be clearly understood by the singer, so that each vowel may be precisely evoked and utilized as a mentally-conceived "control factor", to produce a desire tone.*

There is a *vast difference* between the technical requirements *of the singing voice* and those of *the speaking voice*. It is often *erroneously suggested* that the singing voice and the speaking voice function exactly alike. If this were so, the singer could easily sing any given word clearly and on any pitch, with the same facility and minimal energy, as when speaking. It is important to distinguish between the *instrumental vowels* and the *spoken vowels*. As the singing voice rises in pitch, there is an unavoidable increase in volume, making it increasingly difficult for the singer to maintain *"pure vowels"*. In that case, and to some degree, it is accepted that a compromise in vowel purity is inevitable, in which the vowel's pronunciation is *"modified"*. Presently, excessive vowel modification has become an excuse for the lack of correct structural knowledge and accomplishment. The singer must learn how to bring the five vowels to their purest level of development, while still allowing for the physiological limitations of producing ideal vowels.

The chief focus of any vocal training program must be to establish a primary condition of *upper register dominance* throughout the complete vocal range. The *u (oo) vowel* is best for accomplishing that purpose, as it represents the purest manifestation of the *upper register*, or *"head voice"* register. In its purest form the *u (oo)* vowel is inherently independent from the remaining four vowels, *i (ee), e (eh), o (oh), and a (ah),* and it is detached from all connections to the power factor of singing, or from the "chest voice" register. Take special note that with all vowel examples given in this manual, the classic Italian pronunciation of each vowel, *as pronounced by native Italians*, should be used.

I. The u (oo) vowel

The u (oo) vowel is essentially a *closed vowel.* The terms *"closed" and/or "open"* refer to the various positions of the posterior area of the throat, and the movements that the lips, tongue and cheeks mandatorialy assume. when each of the vowels is *"purely"* pronounced. With each of the five vowels, the singer is obliged to adjust the throat position and the lips and cheeks, according to the particular vowel being presently sung. The *vocal cords* also make difference adjustments, with each individual vowel. The various positions of the throat and the lips, tongue and cheeks range from a fully *closed position,* while singing the *u (oo) and the i (ee)* the two *"closed"* vowels, to a fully opened position of the throat while singing the *a (ah) vowel.*

The u (oo) readily serves to both purify and identify the two registers. The purification process completely separates the muscular actions that produce the u (oo), from all muscular actions of the other four, remaining vowels. Therefore, the *(oo) vowel* helps the singer to eliminate radical muscular conflicts between the *head voice* with the *chest voice. The u (oo) vowel* is the *"headiest"* of all the vowels— whereas the *a (ah) vowel* is the most *"chesty" vowel*—and these polarity differences between them grant the singer a clear comparison of the two registers. This is possible because of the *vast polarity* in the inherent qualities and muscular functions that exist between the two registers, at each extreme. Initially, the qualities of the *undeveloped chest* tones, at the bottom of the singer's range, are *"solid"* and *"resonant", "thick"* and *"weighty"* and *"rigid",* while at *the top* of the singer's range, the qualities of the undeveloped *head* tones are *"soft"* and *"sweet"* and their muscular actions are *"thin", "light"* and *"highly flexible."*

When exercising the voice, the use of the *head voice's* u (oo) vowel permits the singer to readily distinguish all sound qualities and muscular actions related to the *upper register,* from those associated with the different, *though equally important* qualities and muscular actions of the *chest voice.* In the case of the successfully-trained singing voice, neither register's function is ever denied. More significantly, while actually singing, the two registers must come to act together harmoniously and *synergistically;* when coupled together, the registers make possible a voice that could not otherwise exist. However, at the onset of training, it is rather difficult but important to identify and establish the purest muscular action that produce the u (oo) vowel.

The *u (oo) vowel* can serve as a continuous guide (and an effective *"muscular tool"*) for separating the muscles of the *head voice* from those of the *chest voice*, since, by repeatedly performing a series of simple, descending scales, utilizing the u (oo) vowel, they will accomplish the desired separation between the u (oo) vowel, and the four remaining vowel, *i (ee), e (eh), o (oh), and a (ah),* which are essentially dominated by the muscular controls of the *chest voice.*

Similar to the inherent antagonism which exists between the *head register* and the *chest register,* the five vowels, when separated again into *two separate group,* also possess their own form of antagonism toward each other. The two vowel groups are as follows: *Group One* consists of *the u (oo), o (oh) and a (ah) vowels,* which are inherently antagonistic toward *Group Two: the i (ee) and e (eh) vowels.* Other than the u (oo), whenever any of the other four vowels' pronunciation becomes confusing to the singer, the solution to resolving the confusion may be found by placing *the u (oo) vowel* in front of each of the other four, individual vowels, and threading each through the throat socket of the u (oo) vowel.

The ideal order of the vowels

An excellent exercise for understanding the correct sequence of vowels *(meaning a smooth, muscular transition from one vowel to another, on a single tone),* is to start a tone softly with the u (oo), the most important *"tuning" vowel,* and on the same pitch, without taking a new breath, slowly change the u (oo) vowel *(without releasing the breath tension),* to an *i (ee)* vowel, then to an *e (eh)* vowel, then to an o (oh) vowel, and finally to an *a (ah)* vowel. *This is the ideal, permanent order of the vowels,* and performing it results in the maximum harmony of muscular response, which can be muscularly felt, while passing through this precise sequence. If any vowel is removed from this *superior order* and placed in another position, during the passage from one vowel to the other, muscular accuracy and harmony are temporarily denied and disruptive muscular movements will result that cause undesirable sounds.

The ideal passage through the five classic, Italian vowels

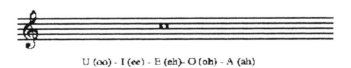

U (oo) - I (ee) - E (eh)- O (oh) - A (ah)

Understandably, when the singer departs from vocal exercises and sings a musical piece, the five vowels are necessarily and unavoidably *"scrambled"* away from their ideal order. Nevertheless, while exercising the voice, to perfect the purity of the vowels, it is essential to maintain this specific *ideal* order, as a standard of reference for each vowel's purity. Because the *u (oo)* possesses an inherent ability to engage the purest and greatest percentage of upper register muscular control, and to disconnect itself from the power of the *chest voice,* when the u (oo) is purely produced, the singer can be sure that all vowels subjected to and transformed by the correct u (oo) vowel's tuning are in their proper register alignment, especially in terms of *"weight"* and *thickness/thinness* evaluations.

Should a *"breathy", "hollow" "muted"* quality appear when using the u (oo) vowel, the singer could easily misunderstand and believe this to be a faulty action. Rather, it is a temporary manifestation of the developing u (oo) vowel *(and to a lesser degree all the other vowels)*, until increased falsetto strength is acquired, following a lengthy period of study, that allows the "core" brilliance of the chest voice to manifest itself with the tone (s) being developed. The singer must remember that it is the u (oo), more than any other vowel, that most resists strengthening throughout the vocal range, especially in the Registers' Break area, and at the lower area of the soprano's range, where the Lower Register's power originates.

During the earlier phases of training, the *u (oo) vowel* often seems to be vague in nature, and a most improbable solution to any problem the singer may encounter, and for correctly structuring her singing instrument, because. And, when the u (oo) vowel is repeatedly evoked, it appears to *"smother"* or *"choke off"* the voice. These are erroneous impressions, and in time and with specific applications, the u (oo) vowel will prove to be one of the most important and *vocalizing and structural tool*. With proper usage, the u (oo) permits the singer to first subjugate the inherent muscular antagonism between the two registers, then reorder these two initially antagonistic forces into a cooperative *"team"* effort. When vocal *"graduation"* draws near, the u (oo) vowel serves *(along with the o (oh) vowel),* to *"round"* and *"polish"* the voice to a professional level, because it alone can guide the accumulated buildup of raw "tonal power", produced by the advanced muscular development of the other four vowels, to a state of smoothness and harmony. It is a tragic fact that, with most present-day teaching methods, *the u (oo) vowel is the least utilized*, most misunderstood, and most wrongly applied *(if at all),* of all the five vowels.

II. The i (ee) vowel

The i (ee) vowel is the second of the five basic vowels that favors the muscular actions of the upper register. In this respect, it is permanently related to the u (oo) vowel. When there is confusion about how to exercise or sing either the u (oo) or the i (ee) vowel, the singer should relate the one that is causing confusion, to the other. This may be done by selecting a *detached, falsetto* pitch and with it, changing from the u (oo) vowel to the i (ee) vowel, then back again to the u (oo) vowel, always on the same pitch, and without taking a new breath. With this exercise, the singer will be unknowingly switching back and forth between the muscular control of the head voice, with the u (oo) vowel passing it head voice control over to the muscular control of the chest voice, with the i (ee) vowel *(this will be explained in detail much later.)* When muscular harmony is attained between these vowels, in the above manner, a superior tone quality appears, and the purity of the *"singing pronunciation"* of the u (oo) and the i (ee) vowels are correct, and so are there *"throat-positions"* appropriately, according the tone and the vowel being presently sung. achieved.

The i (ee) vowel is *(along with the u (oo) vowel),* one of the invaluable *"tuning vowels",* as they were justifiably called during the *Bel Canto* era. This is because both *vowels favor the muscular activities of the upper register*, and they act as a powerful counter-force against the negative influences of the lower register. The correct i (ee) vowel automatically turns itself *upward* and *away* from the bottom of the range *(a factor that I've termed "the inverted tone),* and pulls the selected tone *upward and away from all connections to the lower chest register, when that is desired.* When a tone is operating in the *connected mode, when both registers are operating together,* the *i (ee) vowel*, if purely sung, focuses itself upward, in the opposite direction, from the bottom of the range, and toward the highest tone of the singer's *Top Range.* This automatic "upward positioning" can be used advantageously to engage only the desired muscular actions and qualities of the lower register, by counteracting the *lower register's tendency* to make the voice *"thick"* and *"weighty",* and causing the i (ee) vowel to break away from proper register alignment, particularly while ascending the *vocal tract.*

When attempting to join the two registers together, the tones of the *upper register* frequently resist coupling with the tones of the *lower register, especially at the point of the registers' break.* This may manifest itself by the developing, *detached falsetto i (ee) vowel* breaking away from the singer's attempt to join the two registers together, then *"whizzing"* rapidly upward, toward the top of the singer's range. In a related manner, the tones of the lower register also resist coupling with the tones of the *Upper Register,* breaking away from the upper register and *"falling downward"* toward the bottom of the range.

For a tone to be superior, it must display *beauty of sound, accuracy of pitch, and it must grant the singer absolute control of all intensity dynamics.* To achieve a correct tone's basic *"tilt"* or *"angle of focus",* with all ascending scales and/or vocal phrases, the singer must aim the tone *upward* and *backward toward the upper posterior area of the mouth-pharynx cavity (definitely not "forward and into the mask"),* and toward the top of the range. The falsetto tuning *vowel i (ee)*, when threaded through and u (oo) vowel, or sometimes and o (oh) or a (ah) vowel, guides the singer to this accomplishment. It is advisable for the singer to remain with the *detached falsetto mode* of *the i (ee) vowel,* accessed at the top of her range, for quite some time, before attempting to connect the two registers together. Eventually, as the voice advances in its development, the singer must only employ the advanced developed *falsetto mode* of the i (ee) vowel, to evoke all her *i (ee) vowel tones, and avoid* evoking any i (ee) vowel tones, with the chest voice's muscular controls.

"The mask" (so frequently and wrongly referred to in present-day vocal training), is the "triangular area" of the face that is formed by *the eyes, nose* and *mouth,* behind which are located the *mouth-pharynx* and *the sinus and skull's resonance chambers.* Most present-day students are incorrectly instructed to *"direct a selected tone into the mask",* supported by the false belief that a superior tone can be created directly inside *"the mask"* itself. These directions are too vague. We must assume that what these vocal teachers intend to say is that, the student must first direct the *air flow,* or *motor force* of the "breath stream" toward the vocal cords, and thereafter, direct it into the appropriate resonance chamber, located behind *"the mask".* However, these resonance cavities behind the "mask" *are not the originators of basic tone.* The resonance cavities are only capable of *amplifying and enhancing the sound* of any particular tone, which has first been generated by the vocal cords, located far below these cavities, then vibrations generated by the vocal cords travel upward in the range, riding on the breath flow, toward its appropriate resonance cavity.

The difference between the *incorrect method* of directing the tone *"into the mask",* and the *correct method* of directing the *breath flow upward and backward in the throat,* behind the soft and hard palates, and into the appropriate resonance cavity, is that the latter method guides the singer to sing with a *"loose tongue and lower jaw",* and to discovering the terminal *"hookup points"* of the tones (s). These *"hookup points"* are located at various, specific spots along the posterior "walls" of the mouth-pharynx and head and sinus cavities, which line the resonance channel, as specific places.

The way this operates is that, the singer starts a tone by energizing the vocal cords with breath tension, then she directs the tone *(or more specifically, the vibrations of the vocal cords),* traveling upward on the breath force, backward toward the posterior area of the mouth-pharynx cavity, or to ascending further up the range, behind the soft and hard palates, and toward the tone's appropriate terminal, *hookup point,* located in either the mouth-pharynx or head/sinus cavities, depending on the pitch being presently sung. Therefore, the production of all correct tones must be thought of as a dual-phase operation: *Phase 1,* the generation of the tone by the vocal cords, and *Phase 2, the act of directing the energized, concentrated breath stream, which transports the vibrations of the vocal cords along, backward and upward* toward the selected tone's corresponding *"hookup point",* located within either the mouth-pharynx or head/sinus cavities. Once the tone arrives in its appropriate resonance chamber (and *manifests itself to the singer as an energized, "puffy" stream of breath),* it must be attached to its proper *hookup point* of impingement, to fulfill itself.

These *"hookup points"* will be discussed in greater detail later. Placing a *detached falsetto, head voice u (oo) vowel* or an *i (ee) vowel (which is infused with flowing breath),* in front of any of the other three vowels, when executing an ascending scale, provides the singer with a *"pointer/tuner"* tones which guides the other tones correctly upward and backward in the throat along, the pathway of the ascending vocal scale. The end result of this difficult achievement is traditionally termed *"correct vocal placement".* Utilizing the *i (ee) vowel* tuner *(or in some cases the u (oo) vowel),* is especially beneficial when dealing with a phrase whose starting tones are located within the *registers' break area*. The correct i (ee) vowel, as defined above, will reveal to the singer the precise, desired *tilt* or *angle of focus* of all tones of an exercise or vocal phrase, which originate within the registers' break area.

One hazard of the i (ee) vowel is that it may rapidly attach itself to the *wrong, damaging chest voice muscles* and forced the singer *to incorrectly focus the tone "forward" and* into the front area of the mouth cavity. This must be avoided.

When correctly sung, the correct i (ee) *avoids the front of the mouth cavity* and instead ascends backward toward the upper posterior area of mouth-pharynx cavity, then passes behind the soft palate, *which responds by moving downward and forward*, to clear a passageway for the energized breath force, which is heading toward the resonance cavities of the sinus and skull, within the *Middle, or Top Range*.

If the i (ee) vowel is incorrectly placed, it will immediately break away from its harmonious relationship to the head voice muscles and the moving, energized breath stream. When that happens, the singer will immediately realize that *she has evoked the wrong chest voice muscles*, which immediately stop the *air flow, stiffens her lower jaw, and unavoidably calls into play thick, unmusical, "out of tune" vocal responses*. These factors immediately cause registers imbalances throughout the complete range, and disruptive muscular responses, between various sections of the vocal range, rather than preserving the desired harmony. The incorrect, *"runaway" i (ee) vowel* must constantly be denied, by first starting a selected tone with an u (oo) vowel, then passing on to the i (ee) vowel, without slacking the breath support, or stopping to take a new breath. Accomplishing the above will graphically focus the incorrect, *runaway i (ee) vowel away from all lower connection to the chest voice*, and instead *"loop"* it upward, and into the throat-socket of the head voice's muscular controls, restore the vital breath flow, and correctly direct the tone along the singing pathway. The faulty, chest voice i (ee) vowel must never be allowed to travel incorrectly "forward" into the mouth cavity.

III. The e (eh) vowel

The e (eh) vowel is neither a *"closed"* nor an "open" vowel, as it does not specifically favor the muscular actions of either a *closed lips position of the u (oo) or i (ee) vowel,* nor the open-lips position of the o (oh), or (ah) vowels. The e (eh) vowel involuntarily brings into play *50% of each of the two registers'* muscular influences, thus making it the *"midway"* vowel, situated between the u (oo) and i (ee) vowels, and the o (oh), and a (ah) vowels. As a visual aide, stand before a mirror and sing a comfortable pitch using the "closed lips" u (oo) vowel, then change the u (oo) to the "closed-lips" i (ee) vowel. Stop the tone, take a quick breath, but don't shift your lips-position away from the i (ee) vowel's positioning of them. Then change the i (ee) vowel to the *e (eh) vowel*, noting in mirror that your lips have assumed a midway-position, somewhere between a fully closed-lips position *(which the u (oo) and i (ee) vowels have imposed upon them)*, to a fully open-lips position *(which the o (oh) and a (ah) vowels have imposed on them)*. These same *"closed"*, "midway", and *"fully open"* positions are simultaneously operating with the upper, posterior areas of your throat, simultaneous to, and appropriately with each individual vowel change, as they have been presented above.

As to the various, shifting positions of the posterior area of your throat, it is not possible for you to visualize the differences between their *closed, midway*, or *fully open* positions. Therefore, these positions must be merely mentally perceived. However, they can be very *acutely felt.* These various lips and posterior throat positions are gradually learned, with the progressive development of the two registers, and each individual vowel, since both registers must be made to participate equally in the pronunciation of each vowel, and the precise formation of their corresponding throat positions.

The above experiences will provide an illustration of the complete sequence of throat and lips' positions for all vowels, and precisely clarify the midway position of the e (eh) vowel, situated between the *"closed"* vowels of *u (oo) and i (ee),* and the *"open"* vowels of *o (oh) and a (ah).*

Similarly, the singer should make *mental notes* of the varying posterior throat positions that are engaged while singing the five vowels. The *two "closed" vowels u (oo) and i (ee)* produce a space toward the rear of the throat that feels *"closed"*, with less depth of tone and *"throat space"* available to the singer. When the o (oh) and a (ah) vowels are sung, the singer feels that the space at the posterior of the throat is "open", producing more depth of tone, and with more available "throat space". These sensations are a direct result of the varying percentages of the two registers' muscular proportions, automatically evoked by each individual vowel, when it is purely sung.

Although the e (eh) vowel incorporates equal proportions of the muscular actions of the *upper register* and the *lower register*, it also allows the singer to select, with some facility, the *desired* percentages of the two registers' qualities and muscular actions, when singing a selected tone. The e (eh) could be compared to the fulcrum point of a see-saw. When it seems that a tone is too *"thick"* and *"weighty"*, the singer may tilt the e (eh) vowel tone toward the i (ee) vowel, adding more upper register's influence, while mentally directing the tone backward and upward in the throat. Conversely, when there is a feeling that the tone is too *"thin"* and *"brittle"*, the singer may direct the e (eh) vowel more toward the muscular influences of the more open throated o (oh) vowel.

The e (eh) vowel is often favored by singers with large voices because, more than any of the other vowels, since it keeps the voice's actions, textures and qualities from too much thinning or thickening. The e (eh) vowel most readily allows the singer, with a large voice, a choice of registers' proportioning, according to the vocal need of the moment.

Like the i (ee) vowel, the e (eh) vowel automatically "turns" itself *upward and away from* the Bottom Range, and toward the Top Range. This upward pointing tendency of the i (ee) and e (eh) vowels can most graphically be experienced by performing a few simple, ascending scale exercises with either or both of these vowels, each vowel sung separately of course, from middle C2, and upward in the range, while temporarily neglecting all the tones located below C2.

With the advanced singer who has brought her registers to their fullest development, all correct lips and throat positions are more available than they are to the singer with underdeveloped registers. Therefore, advanced singers are capable of producing purer vowels than those singers with underdeveloped registers. Furthermore, while an advanced singer is singing one particular vowel, of the five available vowels, the purest throat and lips positions of the four remaining vowels *(though not active at the moment),* are readily available, respond quickly, and allow the singer either a slow or rapid change of vowels.

IV. The o (oh) vowel

The *o (oh) vowel* can favor the muscular actions of either the chest register, or the muscular controls of the head register. When the o (oh)'s throat position is modified toward the u (oo) vowel, it favors the head register, and when its throat position is modified toward the a (ah) vowel, it favors the muscular controls of chest register. Should there be any confusion regarding the o (oh) vowel's exact pronunciation and register proportions, this can be clarified by first utilizing the o (oh) vowel, and modifying toward influence of the u (oo) vowel. Then, with a second tone, modifying the o (oh) vowel toward the influences of the a (ah) vowel. When actually singing, this allows the singer another "tuning" advance, since when she feels that the o (oh) vowel of a certain word is becoming overly chest-voice influenced, she can modify it's throat position toward the u (oo) vowel's throat position. And when she feels that the o (oh) vowel of a different word is becoming overly chest voice influenced, she can modify its throat-position toward the (ah) vowel's throat -position. North Americans, in generally, tend to permit the pronunciation of the o (oh) vowel to relate to *the a (ah) vowel.*

The o (oh) vowel may also be utilized to "preset" muscular conditions in the throat to achieve a correct positioning of the a (ah) vowel. This "presetting" technique is essential. The a (ah) vowel is the most difficult of the five vowels to perfect, because it involuntarily pulls into play the maximum activity of the *chest voice,* and therefore, the a (ah) tends to resist proper coordination with the beneficial and protective falsetto's beneficial falsetto action, which also grants the singer the only possible method of dynamic control of the a (ah) vowel. By utilizing the o (oh) vowel to guide the a (ah) into its proper throat position, the difficult a (ah) vowel, which unfailingly tends to respond rigidly and disruptively, may be carefully and exactly placed into its correct "throat space".

When developing a detached falsetto u (oo) vowel, with the *swell and diminish* exercise, especially with a tone in the passaggio area, or within the range of the Top Voice, the singer should mentally and silently arrange the throat position of her u (oo) vowel in a similar position as a silent o (oh) vowel. By while withholding the o (oh) vowel's tendency to increase the tone's volume, the u (oo) vowel can be made to remain stable, while the swelling and diminishing process is being applied, in order to strengthen the u (oo) vowel's throat socket.

V. The a (ah) vowel

The *a (ah) vowel* is the purest lower register vowel. It favors the muscular actions of the lower register *more than any of the other four vowels.* In many cases, the a (ah) vowel favors the chest register *excessively* and *negatively,* so that it tends to exclude the important muscular actions and qualities of the upper register, thereby denying the significant benefits of the u (oo) and the i (ee) vowels, necessary for producing a superior *"rounded", "mellow" a (ah) vowel.* The o (oo) and o (oh) tuning vowels are indispensable, as an aid to preventing the potentially negative activities of the "raw a (ah) vowel" from destroying the correct functions, beauty, and correct *posterior throat-pathway* of all ascending scales and vocal phrases.

The *a (ah) vowel* is the one that most quickly *deceives the novice* into believing that she has achieved strong, superior *"professional tones".* However, they are often incorrect *"chesty"* tones that *will not* let the singer pass through the registers' break area correctly. This frequently made mistake, about the wrongly perceived a (ah) vowels' tones, is usually the results of using the harmful *"Chest Voice Training Method"* of voice production, which relates the singing voice to the speaking voice. This damaging, *"raw a (ah) vowel"* is frequently used in most present-day training programs which employ many ascending scales, using the "unblended" a (ah) vowel, a harmful situation wherein *there is no "binding" or "mixing"* of the a (ah) vowel, with the muscular actions of the developed head register, through the mellowing influence of the u (oo) and o (oh) vowels.

Lilli Lehmann[2] had much to say about: *"the a (ah) vowel of former days".* She said: "the Italians who sing well never speak or sing the vowel sound a (ah) otherwise than mixed, and only the neglect of this mixture *(of the ah vowel, with the head voice vowel u (oo) or o (oh), (author's notes),* could have brought about the decadence of Italian teaching. The incorrect a (ah) vowel can range itself, that is, connect itself, with no other vowel, makes all vocal connection impossible, evolves very ugly registers, and lying low in the throat, summons forth no palatal resonance. The power of contraction of the muscles of speech *(which are evoked by the raw a (ah) vowel— again author's notes),* is insufficient, and this insufficiency misleads the singer to constrict the throat muscles...". From *Lehmann's* marvelous book, *How to Sing.*

In the Fourth Century, the revered *Scuola Cantorum (a musical conservatory in Italy, established by Pope Sylvester, to instruct members of the clergy and the choir on the principles of vocal production*

---

[2] Lilli Lehmann, soprano, born in Würzburg, Germany in 1848, died 1929. She took part in the first complete cycle of Wagner's *Ringes des Nibelungen,* at Bayreuth in 1876. Her London debut was a Violetta, in 1880. In 1885 she made her Metropolitan debut, her roles included Bertha in *Le Prophete,* Margeurite in *Faust,* Irene in *Rienze,* and Venus in *Tannhaüser.* She began teaching in 1981. Her most notable students were Olive Fremstad and Geraldine Farrar.

and musical theory), concluded, after much time and careful investigation, that a singer should be warned against forcing the lower area of the vocal range upward *(by using the wrong a (ah vowel, when it is not connected to the head voice u (oo) vowel—author's notes),* past the point of the registers' break, without employing the requisite amount of *falsetto* or upper register activity to aid the singer to accomplish that daunting task. Essentially, this enlightening *Scuola Cantorum* concept has remained entirely valid, to this day.

When a brilliant *"Italianate" a (ah) vowel* is correctly produced, the sound, *especially with the voices of advanced singers*, can deceive the *uneducated* listener into believing that their a (ah) vowel possesses a great deal of lower register action with it. In fact, the opposite is true; *the correct a (ah) possesses more upper register domination with it, than chest voice domination.* If the singer believes that a near-perfect a (ah) vowel has been achieved, it can be tested by singing a tone with her a (ah) vowel. After stopping to take note of its quality and muscular actions, the singer should start a new tone with an u (oo) vowel, slowly changing it to an o (oh) vowel, and finally to an a (ah) vowel. If her original a (ah) vowel matches the high standards of the new a (ah) vowel, that was achieved by passing it through the u (oo) vowel and o (oh) vowels then, and only then, may the singer say that a near-perfect a (ah) vowel has been achieved.

The five basic vowels, in their purest form, are capable of considerable *(and sometimes unconscious)* modification, so the muscular activities and vocal textures of one vowel may be merged with that of any of the other four vowels. While this adds a rich variety of tonal colors to the singer's vocal palette, it must be kept in mind that *these modifications are deviations from the vowels' ideal pure forms,* and as such they could easily degenerate further from purity. It is therefore imperative that the purity of each vowel be periodically reviewed.

The *motor force of the breath stream,* so necessary for generating all the tones of the complete range, can be partially regulated by the singer through *"vowel modifications".* Meaning that, when a singer establishes a certain note, particularly one in the *passaggio,* and she immediately sense that its *"placement"* is faulty, and has caused a diminishing of the breath flow, or a complete blockage of it, she may adjust the presently sung vowel's throat position by *mixing or "tuning" its throat-position* towards one of the four remaining vowels, other than the one she is presently singing. For example, she can *"tune"* a faltering, overly bright and strident a (ah) vowel, which is negatively effecting the breath flow, toward the "darker" AW vowel. Or, a sluggish o (oh) vowel, which is also negatively influencing the breath flow, towards an u (oo) vowel. These are but a few examples of how *helpfully,* appropriate *"vowel modifications" can be, in order to allow the "breath flow" its complete freedom of passage, up and down the complete range.*

Locating the "Registers' Break"

All sopranos may locate the position of their *"Registers' Break"* by executing a chromatic, eight-tone scale in an ascending direction. Start the scale on Bf below middle C, and with medium volume, ascend the range to the Bf above.

Many individuals tend to argue over the actual location of the registers' break, from their personal point of view, claiming to be right about its location, while all others are wrong. What creates these vast differences of opinions, as to the actual point of the registers' break, is the fact that the muscular behavior of either, or both, registers, when operating within that critical *"transitional area"*, can be altered. In an "altered state", either register gains more/or less advantageous control of the "transitional tones" than the can the other register. If this were not a feasible, it would not be possible for singer to alter and circumvent the problems of the registers' break area, at all!

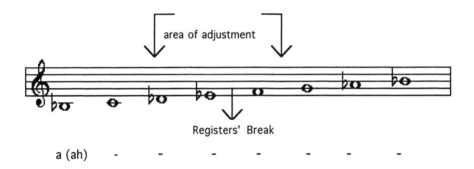

The *above diagram* presents an experimental ascending scale for locating the position of the Register's Break. The a (ah) vowel should be used since it is the most challenging, *and because very few sopranos possess an a (ah) vowel that is correctly blended with the head voice's muscular controls,* within the registers' break area, therefore this experiment may be very revelatory. After the first scale, or one of two more scales may be tried, raising the scale a half tone, then lowering it a half tone.

The register's break is located between E♮ and F♮, above middle C. While proceeding upward from the bottom of the scale, and before reaching the top B♭, the singer will have to make either a major, audible mechanical adjustment, or fail to complete the scale without forcing. This adjustment may occur anywhere between middle C and the F♮ above it. Those singers who can produce an ascending scale as if all its tones were a single muscular unit, of equal quality and dynamics, and with a pure a (ah) vowel, making only minor mechanical adjustments, but still keep a resonant quality, are utilizing a collaboration of the muscular actions of both the chest voice the head voice muscles, to accomplish the ascending scale correctly. Generally, most beginners possess a vocal condition of *divided, and antagonistic registers* which forces them to make a major, audible mechanical adjustment, in order to complete the scale with a resonant quality, beauty of tone, and clear vowels. In most cases, the singer is unable to complete the scale.

The singer with completely harmonic registers is capable of executing an ascending scale rather easily, and without any change of quality, only a minor muscular adjustment as she transfers the breath tension from the lower register, over to the head voice. (Read again: *"The permanent location of the "registers break"— pgs. 11 & 12).*

Never force the Lower Register upward

Never use vocal exercises which force the lower register upward toward, and into the registers' break area. Such counterproductive exercises generally consist of a series of rote, meaningless ascending scales which slur over the much required, detailed analysis, and proper execution of superior tone production. This upward forcing of the lower register is both damaging and highly unmusical, and does not permit the singer to extend her range, with quality tone, further upward than F♮2 natural above C♮2. This method will only end in failure, then other training methods are tried, such as radically reducing the volume of all tones. Or, exercising the voice, solely with one vowel *(usually the i (ee) vowel).* Or *"covering"* the voice *(a method of holding back the brilliance and intensity of the tone which results in a hollow, muffled tonal quality).*

None of these methods will extend the range properly upward. After repeated failures have proven that the lower register cannot be forced beyond E♮ above middle C, the solution to the problems in the registers' break area can be found with the development of the falsetto. Unlike the lower register's tones, the head voice's falsetto tones possess the capacity to be extended in two directions, *upward* and *downward.* With regards to the problems of the registers' break area, the *falsetto must be brought downward to overlap the entire registers' break area, plus the entire lower register. Only then will it be possible to extend the singer's range upward correctly, with superior quality of tone, and without forcing the voice.*

Sopranos, of all the vocal categories, *can least tolerate* the ascending scales that are generally assigned to them. The soprano voice grows from, and finds it best method of approaching exercises *(and singing),* by starting the *"warm-up" or "vocalization"* session with the tones of their *"upper register's break",* more specifically the tones from C2 to the F2 above it.

Kirsten Flagstad, the great Norwegian, Wagnarian soprano said, *"When warming up, I always start with the Middle Range, then descend into the Bottom range, and only after that do I approach the Top Range."*

The most essential element for singing the tones of the lower, *"true" passaggio,* and especially, the high tones above F2, correctly, is the deliberate cultivation of the *head tone,* or advanced developed falsetto, which we refer to as the *mezzo-falso,* or *mixed voice.* The *Top Range* of all female singers' voices, from F♮2 to the B♮2 above it, is the particular area of the singer's complete range where the *air* *flow*s strongest and freest, and the free flow of the breath force is vitally essential for producing *pure, correct "head tones"*. The correct understanding and proper use of this vital *"air flow"* principle is at the core of all *"head voice"* training. This "breath flow" principle has long since disappeared from the vocal studios of the world. Perhaps it was first lost and/or deliberately denied when the falsetto, or the thin, *"whistle voice"*, itself, was no longer considered useful in training the soprano's singing voice. This occurred because most teachers could not reconcile the relationship between the thin, sweet adolescent-sounding *"whistle voice"* and the resonant, powerful *"projecting voice"*, or the traditional performing voice.

Sopranos can hear superb examples of the ways in which the *mezzo-falso or "mixed voice'* is skillfully employed in tone production by listening to the recordings of *Zinka Milanov, Rosa Ponselle, Claudia Muzio* and *Montserrat Caballè*.

Most sopranos can quickly accumulate an extensive *middle range* of tones that are negatively dominated by the chest voice and which *exclude* the proper participation of the head voice. These singers are greatly limited in their use of the *breath force dynamics* and can only sing loudly. They usually excuse their vocal limitation by labeling themselves *"dramatic sopranos"*, as if being a *"dramatic soprano"* *permitted them to dispense with the vocal finesse of "soft tones". When this be the case, it is hoped that the singer will give proper attention to the development of the falsetto's muscular controls, and to overlap all the tones of her chest voice with them.*

In the beginning of vocal training, *with more than 90% of the soprano's vocal range located within the borders of the head voice's influence,* sopranos are well advised to put the strong, vibrant, easily accessible 10% of the *chest tones* aside, *but only temporarily*, and devote their attention to cultivating the *"tiny"* falsetto pitches of the very *Top Range*, known as the *"whistle voice"*. As these whistle-voice tones seem *false* and *unrelated* to the more familiar qualities and muscular responses associated with the performing voice, sopranos usually pay little attention to this sound advice. However, unless these *"seemingly unimportant falsetto sounds"* are cultivated, and brought downward in the range, and made to overlap and dominate all tones from $E\flat2$, then further downward. to the lowest note of her compete range, the singer is inviting a short-lived period of seemingly rapid vocal development, followed by another short period of second-rate singing, that leads to complete vocal failure.

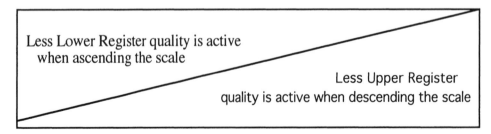

After the two antagonistic vocal registers have been made harmonic with each, each will still retain a considerable amount of its original quality. For example, as the voice *ascends* toward the Top Range, the basic quality of the *lower register* will automatically lessen, to allow the *upper register's necessary participation and positive influence* to come into play. The same rule applies when *descending* toward the *Bottom Range,* the basic quality of the *upper register* will lessen with each descending tone, to allow the *lower register's necessary participation and positive influence* to come into play. When the registers become totally harmonic with each other, this process becomes automatic and *does not* effect the clarity and resonant action of the tones at either extreme of the range. *See the illustration above.*

Subjective and objective perceptions and evaluations of vocal sounds

It has been stated that the singer cannot hear her voice, with the same reality that her listeners can. This suggests that *the singer cannot make appropriate judgments* regarding her own voice, in order to properly structure it. Because of this, the singer decides to collaborate with a voice teacher who is thought to hear the singer's voice with greater perceptive ability than the singer herself. The question then arises: *can a singer, alone, without the help of an "extra pair of ears", foster her own vocal progress?*

The singer *can* help herself to progress vocally, however, a singer's vocal judgments and tonal evaluations, concerning her own voice, must meet rigid standards. Her vocal judgments must be based on her acknowledgment that all vocal sounds, of superior or inferior quality, are symptomatic of what is *physiologically* correct or incorrect. She must carefully evaluate every structural exercise, through *her physical sensations.* Let us call this approach *"feel-hearing".* The singer evokes a tone, for exercise or repertoire purposes, then evaluates the tone that is operating in her throat. A decision is then reached, as to whether or not the instrument's muscles are reacting harmoniously with each other, whether the presently sung vowel is "pure", and is the pitch accurate, and is she mistress of all breath-intensity controls. These strict evaluations can only be reached through *"feel-hearing"* and *not from actually hearing them,* since the student can never hear her own voice, as others do.

The importance of addressing all vocal corrections according to the singer's physical sensations *cannot be stressed enough.*

CHAPTER THREE

Breathing

Where singing is concerned, correct breathing should be referred to as *proper or improper methods of applying the motor force of breath, not* merely *how to inhale and exhale!* Singing requires a greater *energy* demand than *"natural breathing".* At the start of training, the student must develop an "athletic skill" for *drawing in an exaggerated amount of air,* then restraining it within her lungs. By restraining the inhaled breath within her lungs, the singer builds up the necessary *"breath pressure"* necessary to create a substantial "motor force". This *"built up"* breath pressure, when applied properly, takes the form of an energized stream of breath which the singer is obliged to direct against the vocal cords, to produce a selected pitch. There exists a bit of confusion about this procedure, since there are no sensatory nerves in the vocal cords, themselves. Therefore, the singer can only be sure if she is directing the breath stream correctly to her vocal cords, when the tone she has produced can be sounded and easily prolonged, and with a evenness of superior sound.

At the beginning of training, it is necessary to inspire a *larger amount of breath* than later on. In the beginning of training, *much more breath should be inhaled than one would seem is necessary.* Invariably, most beginners feel incapable of accomplishing this task. However, with the progressive development of the vocal muscles, the *exaggerated* amount of breath required at the beginning of training, gradually lessens. This is so because the exercises have accomplished their tasks of fully developing the strength of a given muscle. Consequently the *"work load"* for producing a selected pitch becomes greatly reduced, *but is must not ever be entirely eliminated.* It is for this reason that an advanced singer's *"breathing technique"* seems *"simple and natural".* Despite the many variety of approaches to "correct breathing", there are basically *two methods: "low breathing"* and/or *"high breathing."*

"High breathing" is <u>incorrect</u>

"High breathing" is *incorrect* because it limits the amount of air that can be inspired and denies the complete expansion of the lungs, and an inhalation of the fullest possible amount of breath, to fill them. *High breathing creates* a situation wherein the singer is unable to supply the vocal organ with a sufficient, prolonged flow of air pressure, which is necessary for producing the various notes of her range, especially the higher notes. With *incorrect "high breathing",* which is employed mostly by females, the singer incorrectly raises her shoulders and *pushes the diaphragm incorrectly inward and then upward.* In that way, the lungs are never permitted to *gradually* fill up with air and expand. Consequently, the diaphragm, which is located just below the lowest ribs, *is not* properly lowered and expanded outward, *all around the waist,* to make room for the expanded lungs, as the inhaled air is drawn

into them.

"Low breathing" is <u>correct</u>

With "low breathing", the singer slowly inspires an exaggerated amount of air through the mouth *(never though the nose)*. Properly doing so *lowers the diaphragm*, in order to create space in the chest cavity, for the expanding lungs. Simultaneously, it *extends the* diaphragm *downward* and *outward*, in all directions, around the midsection of the abdomen. After the maximum amount of air has been inspired, it must be held back within the lungs, by resisting the tendency of the diaphragm to collapse inwardly. *Those who cannot grasp the correct method of low breathing usually relate singing to the speaking voice.* This immediately and incorrectly directs the singer's attention *frontally* to the lips, tongue and cheeks. With low breathing, after the lungs have been filled with air, the inspired air is directed at the vocal cords, and the singer must *quickly* seek *the correct pathway for the outgoing breath stream* and direct it at the vocal cords, then into the entrance of the *resonance channel.* This entrance is located at the upper posterior area of the mouth-pharynx cavity.

Nature manifests itself

Long before the average student considers studying singing, her breathing system has been supplying her body with oxygen, necessary for sustaining life, and the motor force for speech. While speaking, air automatically flows into the lungs—*inspiration*—then exits the lungs—*expiration*. While speaking, the air travels tenuously from the lungs along the windpipe, directly toward the vocal cords, which then open and close in *"spurts",* producing the sounds of speech.

The *breath flow* travels this pathway in a self-functioning manner, seldom deviating off the correct path toward the vocal cords, except in unusual situations.

Fig. 1 Female voices

During ordinary speech, at close range, the breath stream travels from the lungs, upward through the windpipe, exits through the glottis *(the opening between the vocal cords),* and oscillates in the lower area of the resonating channel within the range of tones in *figure 1, above.* It settles momentarily upon one pitch, then moves on to another pitch, and so on, until the available breath in the lungs has been used up. Then a new breath must be taken, in order to continue speaking. *But in every case, while speaking, the breath stream seldom rises above the top pitch of B♮.*

While speaking, the breath automatically takes a *wrong pathway,* when compared to the needs of singing. The *breath's wrong path* is more common with English speaking individuals. This is so because the English language possesses a multiplicity of diphthongs *which are a singing disadvantage.* These diphthongs direct the breath stream into the mouth cavity, forward toward the front teeth, then out of the mouth. On the other hand, *the Italian language, the ideal language for singing*, operates almost exclusively on pure vowels, *the so called five "classic Italian vowels" (oo) i (ee) e (eh) o (oh) and a (ah).* These *"pure vowels"* enable the breath stream to rise *above* the top B♮ of the speaking voice's usual range, and into the mouth-pharynx cavity, and in some cases above it, into the head and sinus cavities. and the cavities of the skull.

This is what William Shakespeare, a well known singer and pupil of *Lamperti*, said about this, in his wonderful book *The Art of Singing—1st edition 1899:*

"If the English language taught us sustained sounds, and compelled a loose tongue, as Italian does, we should intuitively possess a higher standard of freedom of tongue and a sense of the open throat. But as the many vowels sounds of the English language are, on the contrary, far less sustained, and, together with our exaggerated, "breath blocking" consonants, lead themselves to a throaty and blurred pronunciation, making the difficulties of prolonging them with open throat, and a loose tongue and lips, still more difficult and apparent, when we try to sing!"

For English speaking individuals, *where classical singing is concerned*, the correct pathway of the "breath stream" *does not automatically* travel a proper route. *Correct singing demands that the singer* is obliged to direct the breath stream far above the top note of the speaking voice's range, of B♮ below *C2.* Therefore, the singer must learn the proper method of directing the breath stream above C^2, then further upward along a specific pathway, which the early master-teachers of singing termed the *Colonna Sonora*, or *the Resonance Channel.*

Along this *resonating channel* there exist various *resonance cavities,* and within them the *"focal points" of impingement for any selected tone,* toward which the breath stream must be directed. When this most important factor about the breath force is totally understood, that of directing the breath force along the length of the resonance channel, and into a specific resonance cavity, it allows the singer to locate the precise *focal point* of the presently sung pitch. Then, in order to develop the strength of that pitch, the singer must gradually increases the amount of breath pressure being applied to that specific *focal point,* in order to fully develop it.

During past great periods of vocal training, these critically important *focal points* were known as the *point d'appui,* by the French *(a point of focus).* And the *punto d'appogiare,* by the Italians, *(a point toward which to direct the breath force).* Utilizing these focal points grants the singer the skill of precise intonation, purity of the *"pronunciation"* of the five classic Italian vowels, plus superior applications of *soft* and *loud dynamics* of the breath force.

The above factors *are seldom considered* in present-day voice teaching. *However, they are of major importance* to a correct program of muscularly building a superior vocal instrument.

CHAPTER FOUR

The "voice building" process & the Vocal Zones

The complete range of tones, available to sopranos of all vocal categories, is by nature subdivided into many smaller groupings. These groups may be referred to as *vocal zones*. Their existence *does not* in any way deny the fact that all the tones of the singer's range are also divided into two major, separate and antagonistic muscular systems: *the upper and lower registers*. The inherent nature of each *Vocal Zone*, its number of tones, and its borders, remain permanently fixed throughout the singer's vocal range, and each *Vocal Zone* obeys the rules that govern the particular vocal register, *upper or lower*, in which it is located.

These Vocal Zones are natural and inherent to the nature of the singing instrument. They are created by permanent muscular subdivisions, that arrange themselves into basic groups; *one group* consists of *five half-tones,* and the *other group* of *seven half-tones.* They contribute greatly to the flexibility of the singing voice, and reveal to the singer a clearer understanding of the singing voice's structural nature. All singers should become familiar with these *vocal zones*, since they play a major role in structuring the *resonance channel.* The complete range of a singer's voice may possess as many as *four (4)* or *five (5) Vocal Zones,* as is the case with some sopranos. The basic characteristics and muscular responses of any, and all of these *Vocal Zones* are determined by their inherent physical structure. Mastery over them is a matter of understanding their individual structure and the technical skill of the singer of controlling each zone.

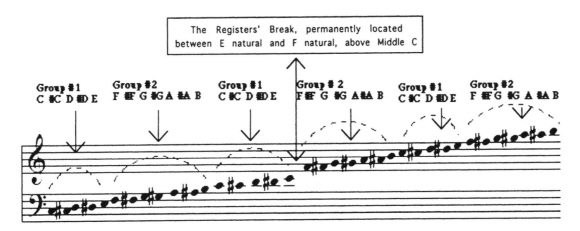

Above is an illustration of the precise and consistent subdivisions of the *Vocal Zones* and the exact pitches that make up each individual group. This pattern is consistent and unalterable.

One of the major tasks of structuring the singing voice is to *"purify"* each Vocal Zone, by eliminating muscular conflicts between any two Zones or more, so that the flowing breath stream, which *"mixes"* with the vibrations of the vocal cords, may pass freely, along the full length of the *resonance channel,* from one Vocal Zone to the next. The existence of these *Vocal Zones* has been observed by many, but most observers believe they are merely *"minor irregularities"* of the complete vocal range, which are of little importance, and can be corrected by merely *"thinking more musically and aesthetically",* when performing vocal scales or phrases. Nothing could be further from the truth. Unless the muscles of each of these individual Vocal Zones is brought to its fullest level of purity and development, it will give the singer great trouble in perfecting her vocal instrument.

Group # 1	Group # 2
C, C#, D, D#, E,	F, F#, G, G#, A, A#, B

The tones located between any particular C♮ and E♮ pitches, and the pitches situated between them *(from any particular section of the singer's complete range),* all have but one muscular control, and they belong to the same Vocal Zone, named *Group # 1*, for convenience. All the tones of *Group #2* have but one mutual muscular control. All the pitches of each individual Vocal Zone respect all the muscular attributes, characteristics, and muscular controls of the *particular vocal register* in which they are located. The tones of C♮ and E♮, at each end of the *1st Zone*, are the *"framing" or "border tones"*, and C♯, D♮, D♯ are the *"central pitches"* of the *1st Zone*.

The tones located between any particular F♮ and B♮ pitches, and the pitches situated between them *(from any particular section of a singer's range),* belong to the same vocal zone, named *Group #2*, for convenience. These tones have but one mutual muscular control, while still respecting all the muscular attributes and tonal characteristics of the *vocal register* in which they are located. The tones of F♮ and B♮, at each end of the Zone, are the "framing" or "border tones", and F♯, G♮, G♯, A♮, and A♯ are the *"central pitches"* of this 2nd group.

These Vocal Zones obey a precise and consistent formation—one following immediately after the other, in exact repetition—*regardless of the singer's individual vocal category.* With experience, it is revealed that *the tones closest to the middle of any particular vocal zone* respond more readily to vowel purity and muscular strengthening, than do the border tones. Also, the *central tones* respond more positively to an increase of breath pressure, than do the tones at both ends of that zone. Therefore, it is advisable to initiate most vocal exercises, using the tones that lie toward *the center* of any given vocal zone.

When a singing voice gets into trouble, due to *"strained singing"* or faulty structuring procedures, the purity of one or more vocal zones' muscular interactions, with one of its neighboring zones, has been disturbed, and *no vocal rest period will restore these zones to their proper order.* To accomplish restoration of vocal health and *Vocal Zone purity*, the singer can apply a series of single, sustained tones, to any impure tone, utilizing the ideal progression through the five vowels exercise *(p. 29)*, strictly retaining their superior order, and all five vowels are to be sung on the same pitch, without taking a breath between each vowel. If any *"jam-ups" or "knots"* exist along the singer's complete vocal range—a situation where one zone's muscular actions have been forced upward or downward out of its rightful territory, and into another neighboring zone's territory—the ideal progression through the five vowels will begin to restore muscular order and vocal health. *(I have written extensively on the subject of "Vocal Zones" in my 1995 vocal manual, A Singer's Notebook) .*

The preferred register for starting vocal exercises

For the first vocal exercises *(p. 49),* it is best to select a *detached falsetto tone* from the Top Range because *"the falsetto" or "whistle voice"* has generally been neglected in that area of the range, and the tones' falsetto muscular controls have remained undeveloped. These "top" tones allow the singer to readily access the flow of the "breath force", which is very important when transporting the head voice's muscular influence downward in the range.

One of the many difficulties encountered, when taking information and vocal exercises from a manual, is that the singer evaluates new information based upon her own, personal vocal experience, and present vocal condition. *From a psychological point of view*, this exerts an enormous influence upon how new ideas are received and utilized. *From a psychological point of viewpoint,* the individual's vocal muscles have already been trained in a certain way, and respond accordingly, so that *new arrangements* are not easily nor quickly accomplished. To achieve the maximum benefit from all the information presented in this manual, the singer should periodically review her own personal vocal history, so that it can stand ready for comparison to the new, perhaps contradictory information being presently studied.

It is important to clarify why the first exercises scales must be executed *exclusively* in a *descending direction. The descending scale pattern tends to negate the negative factors of the chest voice, while enhancing the purification of the upper register, so that all its tones become muscularly harmonious with one another, and free from any negative relationship with the chest register.* In this *"pure"* state, the *upper register* can be said to be *"detached"* from the solid, vibrant action of the chest register. In this *"pure, detached state"*, these descending upper register scales can be made to encompass then muscularly influence *all the tones* of the singer's complete vocal range.

While descending the vocal range with these first exercises, the singer will arrive at the registers' break *(between E♮ and F♮ above middle C)*. At that specific point, the singer must continue downward in the range, past the registers' break, *without shifting the muscular control of any pitch away from the upper register's muscular control,* over to the lower register's muscular control. Instead, the singer must "*stretch*" the upper register's muscular controls downward in the range, and over the *passaggio* tones, in an overlapping manner.

When approaching the *passaggio* tones, the singer whose both registers are *antagonistic toward each other* will experience a tendency of the voice to *"break"* away from the upper register's muscular control, and snap downward, into the muscular controls of the lower register. This must not be allowed. This *undesirable breaking away* is due to the fact that, at the point of the registers' break, the lower register's muscular controls are *strongest,* while at that same point, the upper register's muscular controls are *weakest.* By the singer firmly insisting upon descending the range and maintain the muscular controls of the *upper register, even if the sound of the tones is less than ideal, and the muscular sensations seem "unnatural" and "cramped",* she is taking *the first major step* towards *"registers blending"*. The best way to avoid surrendering the head voice dominated, descending scale over to the muscular controls of the lower register is for the singer *to reduce the volume of these passaggio-crossing tones* to a minimum dynamic, and to use the two "headiest vowels", *u (oo)* and/or *i (ee),* for these first descending scale exercises.

Unlike the *lower register, which is "square , inherently rigid and inflexible,* the *upper register* is *"round" "supple" and "flexible"*. The *upper register* possesses a phenomenal capacity to be *"stretched"* downward and cover all the tones of the *lower register* with its muscular controls. Doing so will gradually alter and transform all chest voice's pitches *away from their original "chest voice dominance", and give them over to "head voice's" muscular influence. This "stretching downward process" takes a long time to accomplish its total goal.* The muscular controls of the *upper register* can *also be extended upward* to the highest pitch in the singer's range, that sound *musical judgment* permits. On the other hand, the *lower register* is inherently restricted, and can only be made to ascend to E♮ above middle C, although that is not desired. At E♮ above middle C the undesirable, rising chest register reaches *an impasse.* Beyond that point, *"power"* and *"resonance"* can only be extended further upward in the range by force, but with detrimental consequences for the entire vocal instrument.

All ascending, *head voice* scales urge the singer to join the action of the lower register to the upper register. This is so because, with each rising tone the vocal instrument *cannot* sustain the continuously increases of breath tension that are undeniably demanded by the voice, without the help of the chest voice; therefore, the *lower register* is automatically pulled into action, the two registers unite, then together they accomplish the tasks of the ascending scale. *It is for this reason that we exclusively use the descending direction pattern, with all the scales, during the first phase of structure, in order to reduce lower register's participation to a minimum.*

THE FIRST VOCAL EXERCISE: *The single, sustained, detached falsetto tones*

The first vocal exercise is the single, sustained, *detached falsetto tone*, performed with tones that are selected from the *Top Range,* F2 to the B2 above it.

The exercises above should be performed with the *detached falsetto "head voice" vowels u (oo)* and *i (ee), and in a descending direction.* Then *much later* they should be performed again, using the *e (eh), o (oh),* and *a (ah)* vowels. The keys of these exercises should be lowered by half tones, until the exercises include more pitches of the *Bottom Range.*

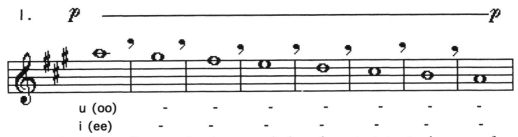

The premise of these first exercises is to start the long, important structural process of *"transporting"* the muscular controls of the upper register downward in the range. The goal is to make as many muscular discoveries as possible, derived from the physical sensations felt when descending from the *Top Range* toward the *Middle Range* and descending further towards the *Registers' Break.* It is critical to maintain the upper register's muscular controls as far downward into the lower range as is possible. The *u (oo)* and *i (ee)* vowels will help to purify the upper register's action, thereby eliminating muscular conflicts.

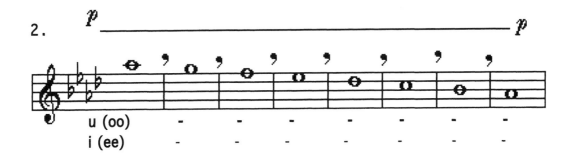

3.

u (oo) - - - - - - -
i (ee) - - - - - - -

The beginner is expected to produce the vowel as purely and precisely as possible, while accompanied by *a free flow of the breath stream*, remembering to diminish the volume of the presently sung tone (s) at the approach to the registers' break. Arriving there, one possible physical observation which the singer may make is that, these *falsetto* tones "shrink" in *throat space* and become *"closed"* and/or *"squat"*, as the singer approaches the "break area", and to a greater degree, once the singer descends *below "the registers' break"* and enters into the lower register. These *"shrinking"* and/or *"closing"* sensations are natural responses. The above *compromises to the vowels* and the *"throat-spaces"* also reveal the inherent muscular contours *(or shape)* of the registers, at the point in the range where they meet each other, which is between E♮ and F♮ above middle C. Later on, we will discuss how to alter these contours of the registers' break area to a different structure that enables the singer to pass through the registers' break with superior tone quality, full control of all breath dynamics, and vowel purity.

These first descending scales also serve to reduce the *"weight"* and *"bulk"* of the lower register, by holding back its volume and allowing the "falsetto" muscles to dominate all its tones.
Because of the variety of conditions in which singing voices are frequently found, the singer should experiment with all the vowels, when performing these first exercises. By referring back to the *"The Mechanical Functions of the Five Singing Vowels" (p. 27*), and reviewing how each vowel may possibly react to these various exercises, the singer becomes more familiar with the muscular sensations and tonal attributes of this critical section of her complete range, while in her present state of development. In this way, she will be able to compare and evaluate how they change after each new structural exercise has been applied, and how her voice has been improved.

Many individuals mistakenly believe that a singer's vocal category is based solely upon the initial *"color"* and/or *"timbre"* of her voice. However, the real basis upon which a singing voice is correctly categorized is by learning about the inherent size and strength of the muscles of both vocal registers. "Dramatic" and *"spinto"* sopranos possess inherently larger-sized lower register muscles than upper register's muscles. *"Lyric"* and *"coloratura"* sopranos possess inherently *larger upper register muscles* than lower register muscles.

These first structural exercises deal with *"detached falsetto"* tones, which possess no *vibrato action. The vibrato* action is derived from the vocal cords, and with these first exercises the singer and teacher will be dealing with tones that *do not* possess any strong *"vibrant", "projecting"* power that is generally associated with a fully developed, professional voice. The suspension of judgment during this period of training is one of the most important factors for eventually attaining a superior singing instrument. It is also a test of the singer's patience and her logic.

Specific, detailed explanations will be provided later, that clarify how the upper register's tones become gradually transformed, and how they allow for an accurate determination of the singer's true vocal category. The determinants for vocal categorization will be the *"weight"* of the voice, and the number of notes that can be drawn from the lower register's *"power system"* and added to the complete range, while maintaining evenness of vocal tone, throughout the entire range, with clear, pure vowels, beauty of tone, and complete control of all breath dynamics.

While these first falsetto exercises start in the *Top Range*, F2 up to B2, with the intention of first establishing the purest *"head tone"*, some sopranos find them rather difficult to access, in their extremely *soft, detached falsetto form*, and instead, they find that a *"stabbing" fortissimo"* approach is much easier, for accessing them. That is because their *Bottom Range* is either undeveloped, or *weighted down* with negative chest voice. When that be the case, the primary structural priority should be given to the *Middle and Lower Ranges*. First the *middle range*, starting an exercise with the E♮2 above C2, then descending the range below the B♮ below C2. Then work with the *bottom range*, from B♭ below C2, descending as far down as downward in the range as B♭ below middle C. This does not suggest that, the singer should not occasionally try to once again to access the detached falsetto with the tones of her Top Range, which had earlier given her difficulty in accessing them.

There exists an unusual *"seesaw"* pattern, necessary for effectively exercising *all female voices*. By alternating the application of exercises between the tones of the lower extreme, between middle C, and the E♮ *above* it, then resting the voice for a few hours or even a day, then exercises the complimentary tones of E2♮ downward to the F♮ *bellow* middle C, faster progress may be had. *Clarification of this theory later on.*

Technical insights into the lower range of all female voices

Correct vocal structuring of the *above four zones* of the soprano's range *(page 45)*, is critical at the onset of training. For example, when the voice is classified as a *lyric soprano,* appropriately so, or not, the tones of the *bottom of the range* are frequently underdeveloped.

They lack strength and core brilliance, and they are often *"sweet", "thin",* and *"breathy",* and lack interesting *"tonal character"*. The singer possesses little dynamic control of these lower tones, with only the softness dynamic available to her. In this underdeveloped state, the voice does not reveal anything special about it, nor its true potential, until the singer reaches the C2, the start of her *Middle Range,* and further upward in the range.

Figure # 1   Figure # 2

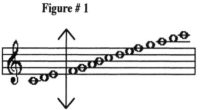

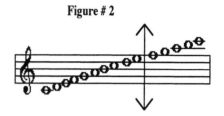

The actual location of the female registers' break, situated between E and F natural above Middle C.

The frequently __mistaken__ concept of where the female registers' break is located, between E and F natural, above C-2.

When the singer is classified as a *dramatic soprano,* or *spinto* soprano *(a vocal classification in-between "dramatic" and "lyric"),* her lowest tones are generally strong, but wrongly so, while her *Middle Range's* tones are inappropriately *"dark"* and *"strong" but* raw sounding, and difficult to control. And, with her *Top Range*—F2 to B2—her tones are frequently *"shouty",* with inconsistent *"hit and miss"* attacks. The Top Range tones, which give all "heavy voiced" female singers a great deal of trouble, lack *focus, brilliance* and *vowel purity,* and they often *"crack"* or *"wobble",* especially when attempts to sing the a (ah) vowel. This voice is a classic example of "the singer with a hole in the middle of her range".

With both these vocal conditions, the problems with the tones from E♮ above C2 downward to middle C of the lower range, can be corrected by overlapping the qualities and muscular controls of the *head voice tones* over all of them, with a full flow of the breath force, then continue downward to the lowest tones of the range.

It is important to understand that none of these above mentioned of the *upper passaggio* and Top Range tones will come to possess *"core brilliance", "pure vowels",* and control of the *breath dynamics, until after* the problematic lower *"true" passaggio* has been properly structured, which take quite a long time to accomplish. This fact is *emphasized,* because most female singers, can get by for a while, by leaving the lower of octave of her range *undeveloped* for a long time, but eventually this neglect shut down her entire voice. Many female singers are also *confused or mistaken* about the actual location of the *true* registers' break. For all female voices, it is located between E♮ and F♮ above middle C. The E♮ above middle C belongs to the *lower register,* and the F♮ above middle C belongs to the *upper register.*

Concerning *mezzo-sopranos* and *contraltos.* Presently there appears to be an overabundance of both categories, but in truth they are actually sopranos *who have not developed* their top, head voice register to its fullest. "Authentic" *mezzos* and *contraltos are rare voices, indeed.*

The beginner is expected to produce the vowel (s) as precisely as possible, which can best be achieved by diminishing the volume of the tones at the approach to the registers' break. As the singer descends the range with these detached "falsetto" tones, and arrives at the registers' break, the singer may observe that the tones "shrink" in throat-space and become rather *"closed-throated"* and/ or *"squat."* And once she descends further in the range, below the registers' break, these tones "shrink" and "close", to a greater degree. These compromises to *"vowel purity"* and "throat space" also reveal to the singer possibly new muscular contours of the registers at the point of the register, which will eventually allow her to pass back and forth through the *break area*, with superior tone quality, dynamic control, and pure vowels.

Regarding the exercises on *pages 49 & 50*, for the pitches of all these exercises to muscularly harmonize with each other, and produce a smooth, even scale, the singer must understand the differences between *ascending* and *descending* vocal movement. *Any and all ascending vocal movement* automatically tend to join the muscular actions of the lower register, to the muscular actions of the upper register. This is so because, with each rising tone of an ascending scale, the vocal instrument demands an appropriate increase of breath tension. The upper register, working alone, *cannot sustain these increases of breath energy,* being undeniably added to each successive, higher pitch. Therefore, the lower register is automatically and undeniably pulled into play, in order to help the head voice's muscles counter-resist the incremental increases the breath pressure. Only when the two registers operate together as a team, in this manner, can the ascending scale be smoothly and correctly executed.

Conversely, any *descending movement* automatically *decreases the amount of breath pressure* necessary to produce the *descending direction* of the scale. Therefore, by incrementally decreasing the amount of breath pressure being applied to each lower pitch of the descending scale or vocal phrase, it automatically diminishes the percentage of lower register participation with each lower pitch of the descent.

By now, the singer should be able to evaluate many of positive structural changes that have occurred with her singing voice, such as, increased muscular harmony between the two registers. To discover further evidence of positive changes, the singer should test the purity of her vowels, and her control of the dynamics from soft to loud.

Vowel throat-sockets

Each individual vowel conveys to the singer a mental concept of its *"vowel throat-socket"*, and the manner in which it is formed and positioned in her throat. *Each vocal register* conveys to the singer *its own set of vowel throat-sockets*, plus an individual tone's muscular controls, which obey certain rules that are indigenous to that particular pitch and register. *Each and every combination of pitch and vowel* of the singer's complete range, has its own vowel throat-socket. By making all of the *upper register's throat-sockets the dominant muscular control factor throughout the complete range,* then stressing each tone's throat-socket, each individual tone may be developed to its maximum. In that advanced state of development, the singer can relate *the vowel throat-socket of an upper register tone, to the corresponding vowel throat-socket of the lower register.* In that way, she may clearly vision the proper method of connected both upper tone's vowel throat-socket together to the corresponding lower tone's throat socket, by swelling the *top tone's* vowel's throat-socket, until it pulls the lower vowel throat-socket up to it, allowing the singer to connect both upper and lower vowel throat sockets to each other. Successfully achieving accomplishing this, with each individual pitch of the singer's complete range, is very difficult and time consuming.

Each vowel exerts its individual, lower register influence upon a tone

Each individual vowel automatically *increases* or *decreases* the lower register's percentage of muscular influence upon a selected tone, whether that particular tone be a *lower, middle,* or *top register* tone. This can be graphically understood by selecting a tone from either the *lower, middle,* or top range, and performing with it, a passage from the u (oo) vowel, then to the i (ee) vowel, then the e (eh) vowel, the o (oh) vowel, and finally the a (ah) vowel, without stopping to take a new breath. This precise order *represents the permanent harmonic order of transition through the five vowels, starting with the u (oo) vowel, passing to the i (ee) vowel, then to the e (eh) vowel, then to the o (oh) vowel, and ending with the a (ah) vowel.* When changing from one vowel to the next, the singer will notice that, there automatically and undeniably occurs an increase of lower register's muscular participation, with each successive vowel, and a change with the vowel throat-socket's space and size. This rule applies to all vocal states in which the vocal instrument may be found, whether that state be one of *upper register dominance*, or of *lower register dominance,* or the *ideal state of harmoniously-structured registers.*

Once the singer leaves the first vowel, the u (oo) and changes to the i (ee) vowel, there occurs an automatic and undeniable increase of the lower register's muscular participation with the selected tone. A further increase occurs with the e (eh) vowel, and still more with the o (oh) vowel, until the a (ah) vowel is reached, *where maximum participation* of the lower register occurs. The throat-socket space evoked by each individual vowel changes from smaller to larger, and/or less throat-socket space and/or more throat-socket space, appropriate to the particular vowel being presently sung.

For theoretical purposes, let us assign each vowel—*after departing from the u (oo) vowel—the purest, and most "detached from the chest voice power"* of the five vowels—a *25% value*, so that the total of these four vowels makes up 100% of the lower register's total potential contributions. Although these percentages may not be precise, undeniably, *there does occur* a considerable increase of lower register participation, with each vowel change. The *reverse* is true when singing a tone that is started with the a (ah) vowel, when the fullest connection of the lower register to the upper register is operative, and the widest vowel-throat space is formed. With the a (ah) vowel, the "work-load" is at its highest level. When the singer changes the a (ah) vowel to an o (oh) vowel, then an e (eh), then an i (ee) arriving finally at the u (oo) vowel, the singer can graphically understand *(and feel),* the gradual incremental decreases of the lower register's muscular participation, which has occurred with each successive change to the new, lower pitch and vowel.

The u (oo) vowel	=	0%	of lower register muscular participation.
The i (ee) vowel	=	25%	of lower register muscular participation.
The e (eh) vowel	=	50%	of lower register muscular participation.
The o (oh) vowel	=	75%	of lower register muscular participation.
The a (ah) vowel	=	100%	of lower register muscular participation.

The above principles can be useful as *vocal imagery* to guide the singer in temporarily isolating certain aspects of vocal, muscular behavior. This will help clarify each vowel's individual nature, and how each vowel can be muscularly developed, and the critical role each vowel plays "separately" from the others, or, when "combined" and "coordinated" with other organs and maneuvers of the vocal instrument.

The *beginning singer* should not become anxious if all this seems complex and overly mechanical. With repeated references *to,* and subsequent applications *of* these important principles, regarding the vowels and their individual throat-sockets and how they activate varying percentages of the upper or lower register participation, and their corresponding *larger* or *smaller throat-sockets*, all will become easier to understand.

THE SECOND VOCAL EXERCISE:
Descending falsetto scales that includes vocal movement

After a certain period of applying the first exercise—*The Single Sustained Tones*—has past, the singer is ready to perform exercises that include *vocal movement*. This leads to the *second basic exercise*: *Descending, Detached Falsetto Scales* that include vocal movement.

The purpose of the new exercises is twofold: *1st)* to gain experience with vocal movement; *2nd)* to overlap the detached falsetto tones' muscular influence downward in the range, temporarily denying the lower register's natural vibrato action. To achieve this, the singer must infuse all of these descending scales with a ample flow of breath, selected from the Top Range.

Applying these "breath-flow", descending-scale exercises may cause the singer some confusion and feelings of insecurity. Many frustrated singers resist the use of these exercises, because when the average singer is denied *the solidity and vibrancy of the lower register*, she feels discouraged and vocally *"lost"*. However, the *"vagueness"* of the *"falsetto voice"* is only temporary and necessary, in order to allow the lower register's muscles to undergo a major transformation in which its *"bulk and rigidity"* become eliminated, and all the lower register's tones have become harmonious and cooperative with the muscular controls of the upper register.

With the further passing of time, *the detached falsetto exercises* may create an impression that, the voice is being *muffled*, or described more traditionally, *"covered"*, and at the same time, producing undesirable *"somber timbers"*, as the old master teachers called them. This greatly misunderstood *"covered feeling"* will eventually spread downward, throughout the singer's *Middle* and *Lower Range*, but these *somber timbers* become especially apparent, in the form of *"a veiled quality"*, with the all the tones that are situated just above the *lower, true* registers' break—F♮, F♯, G♮, and G♯ above middle C.

This *"veiled quality"*, is perceived more by the singer, than by her listeners. *It must not be sacrificed* by inappropriately attempting to restore *core brilliance to the above mentioned tones.*

With great patience, and continually applying the detached falsetto voice and the *messa di voce exercise,* these frustrating, confusing *"covered", "dark timbered"* falsetto tones will arrive at an advanced state of development *and* the *missing core brilliance* and projecting power will emerge, but in a new, correct, permanent form—that of being *"mixed voice tones".* *Mixed voice* tones are initially created from a mixture of the *breath stream's energy* and *the vibrations of the vocal cords.* In their *"mixed state",* these advanced developed tones will grant to the singer *flexibility, control* of *all dynamics, pure vowels,* and a *professional quality of tone, throughout her entire range.*

The singer must be open-minded, during the long transition through *this "covered' or "closed" phase* of vocal training, until the *"mixed voice"* appearance. She must understand that, the former, readily available, tangible characteristics of the lower register *were incorrect and misleading raw chest tones,* and that, had she maintained them in that incorrect form, they would have denied her the attainment of a superior, synergistic *(a condition wherein the two registers are connected to each other),* vocal instrument.

The singer who *has not followed the above procedures* of applying exercises *1 & 2* and has not passed through the first *"covered phase,* has instead surrender her voice over to the negative volume and bulk of the "unblended", "raw" chest register, and she will eventually discover that that was *all wrong*! But sadly, only after her singing voice had totally failed her! She shoulder then summon up courage and submit her singing voice to the therapeutic influences of the detached falsetto exercises. If she does, she will quickly come to appreciate the detached falsetto's *"soothing, positive, restorative",* influences upon her singing voice more strongly than other sopranos, who *have not* experienced her first, "faulty" unproductive, "chest voice" start.

Where proper vocal structuring procedures are concerned, *a little knowledge of the falsetto voice and its principles is not only dangerous, but baffling and frequently destructive.* One must possess total knowledge of the various phases of development, through which the falsetto voice passes. Most popular, present-day *misconceptions and consequent rejections* of *falsetto voice training* are mainly due to *partial knowledge* of the falsetto's complex training procedures, and the fact that, the falsetto can appear to be vague and harmful when misused.

Legato: The meaning of the term "legato"

With the addition of vocal *movement* into the exercises, the term *legato* must be explained. Traditionally, *legato* is thought of as a method of closely connecting two or more tones when passing from one to another, so as *not* to allow any *audible gaps* in the sound, between them, to occur. This *is certainly one of the rules* of legato singing, *but* there exist many more. Most singers fail to consider the causative agents that achieve *legato*, and have no understanding of its muscular requirements.

Exercise scales generally employ but a single vowel. To the contrary, a vocal phrase contains many vowels *"scrambled"* into the text, *out of their ideal order, which is—u (oo), i (ee), e (eh), o (oh), and a (ah)*. Therefore, achieving *"smooth legato"* while applying a vocal exercise is a different matter than when actually singing a particular phrase of a musical piece, which presents a much greater challenge. During the execution of a selected vocal exercise or phrase, while passing from one pitch to the other, the force of the breath pressure, which creates basic the tone or tones involved, must not be slacked off or totally dissipated. With excellent legato, the breath force, established on the first tone and its particular vowel, must be momentarily reduced then quickly transferred to the second tone *and its particular vowel,* without losing the breath-force being applied to the vocal cords. Much skill is required in diminishing and increasing the breath force, when passing from one tone to the next, but never allowing it to stop for a moment.

Changing from one pitch to the next, and not losing breath force is made even more complicated when the vowel of the first tone is different from the vowel of the second tone. Physiologically, this means that the first vowel's *throat-socket* is different from the second vowel's *throat-socket,* and achieving a perfect match of these different throat-spaces, while keeping the breath flowing, is a more complicated a matter. Since each of the five classic vowel, *u (oo), i (ee), e (eh), o (oh), and a (ah)'s* throat-sockets alters and adjusts the throat-socket of the presently sung tone, from slightly open—to medium opening—to fully opening, the manner in which the singer manages the continuous flow of the breath force, while changing the pitch and vowel and *throat socket*, determines her skill in accomplishing *"smooth legato"* while singing.

Legato is *only* possible when *each tone* in the singer's complete range has been individually strengthened to a state of muscular perfection. In such a state, no tone is weak or incapable of *transferring* or *receiving* the motor of the breath-force, nor adjusting a tone's throat-socket from one vowel throat position to another, but different, vowel throat-position.

1) Every tone of the complete range must be strengthened individually, and separately from all the others.

2) There exists a difference in legato application when performing an *ascending scale* which automatically increases the amount of breath pressure applied to the vocal cords, than when performing *a descending scale* which automatically demands a decrease of breath pressure, being applied to the vocal cords.

3) The vowels employed on the adjacent tones of a selected pitch have a critical influence upon how the singer accomplishes the transfer of the breath tension from one tone to the next, since each new vowel creates a different size throat-aperture through which the air must pass through, on its way producing the selected tone. There is greater challenge to maintaining legato when one of the pitches possesses an *"open" vowel—a (ah) or (oh)—*and *the other pitch a "closed" vowel, such as—u (oo) or i (ee). The u (oo), o (oh) and (ah) vowels* create a *"more open"* throat aperture than *the i (ee) and e (eh) vowels*, therefore they grant the singer a fuller *"breath flow".* The i (ee) and e (eh) vowel, create a "more narrow" throat aperture, than *the u (oo), o (oh), and a (ah) vowel,* and therefore they grant the singer a lesser amount of "breath flow".

Note: With some of the above situations the *"portamento "*is frequently used. This is a method by which *the singer carries the vowel of the first tone of a phrase upward to the second tone,* and only then changes to the second, different vowel.

4) The distance between two pitches of a vocal phrase critically affects the manner in which correct *legato* can be accomplished. It is more difficult to maintain *legato* when singing *a widely-spaced interval* than it is with *a closely-spaced interval.* This again involves proper management of the breath force and rapid adjustments of the different vowel throat-sockets, between the two pitches that are involved.

The "two passaggios" theory held by many female singers

Before presenting the *Second Exercise,* it is important to discuss the *popular misconception* held by most female singers that there exist two passaggios *(or register breaks),* within their complete range of tones. According to this "theory", the *first break* is located between E♮ and F♮ above middle C, at the lower end of the range. And the *second break* is located between E♮2 and F♮2 above C♮2, toward the upper middle of the range. This "two breaks" theory *is incorrect. There is but one authentic "register break" and it is* located between E♮ and F♮ above middle C, at the lower end of the complete range. *(See pg. 12).*

Because more than two-thirds of the female vocal range lies above the *"true"* lower registers' break, it is difficult for female singer to transfer the *vibrato action* of the vocal cords upward in the range, to the tones to the *upper middle* of the range, situated between F♮ and E♮ above C2. The tones of both the *lower* registers' break" and the *upper* registers' break are highly reflective of each other's *positive* or *negative* states of development. From now on, for convenience, we will refer to *the true, lower register break* as the *"lower break",* and the inappropriately called *upper* register's break, between E♮ and F♮, as the *"upper break."*

If the problems of the *lower break* go unresolved, it will always prohibit the singer from transferring *vibrant power* upward to the *Middle and Top Range's* tones. This is because the *"true"* break's tones form an *impasse, for the breath flow and the vibrations of the vocal cords.* I have named this *impasse* the *"vocal chasm"*, which *blocks the air flow from transporting the vibrant vibrations of the vocal cords* (traveling upward along the resonance channel), from passing freely into these range areas. Once all the tones of the *"lower break"*, have been properly structured, the *impasse* of the *vocal chasm* will have been removed and the breath flow will travel freely through the "chasm" and allow the vocal cords' vibrations to reach the Middle and Top Ranges.

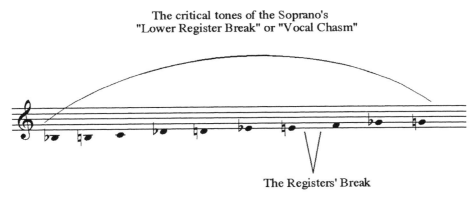

The critical tones of the Soprano's
"Lower Register Break" or "Vocal Chasm"

The Registers' Break

Accomplishing the structural transformation of the *vocal chasm's tones* involves two separate phases. With the *lst Phase,* by performing many soft, descending, detached falsetto scale exercises, using the open i (ee) falsetto vowel. An open, detached falsetto i (ee) vowel can be accessed by establishing the *throat position* of a silent, *unsung* a (ah) vowel, then actually singing the open, detached falsetto i (ee) vowel, which must retain the open throat position of the a (ah) vowel. A great deal of breath pressure must flow through the tone, while attempting to establish the open i (ee) vowel. And, while doing so, *the tongue* must be moved upward, out of the lower throat channel, and into the mouth cavity. Once positioned inside the mouth cavity, the tongue's *middle section* should rise upward toward the *hard palate* and form a mound, while the tongue's tip should be loosely positioned behind the lower front teeth.

After performing the *lst phase of structuring the vocal chasm—the* soft, descending scales exercise, *and for quite a long time,* all *the chasm's tones* must be strengthened individually, one by one, by performing the 2nd Phase.

With the 2nd Phase, perform the *swelled tone exercise,* with the intention of pulling the chest's voice power smoothly upward from below and connecting it to each starter-tone of the vocal chasm.

First perform the exercises below, in preparation for the exercises that follow afterward.

Descending, soft exercises for the Sorpano's "lower Registers'

open i (ee) vowel --

Now perform the exercises below

Swell and Diminish exercises for all soprano's lower range

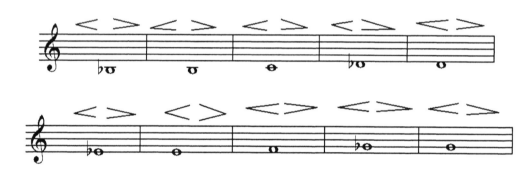

When performing the *swell and diminish* exercises of the above pitches of the lower range, using the open i (ee) detached falsetto vowel, the singer must first establish a *silent*, full throated a (ah) vowel, throat-position and then place the open i (ee) vowel, which will be actually sung, in the center of the silent, full-throated open a (ah) vowel's throat position.

One negative, though temporary result that could occur, after performing many of the above exercises, is that entire lower range, from F♮ above middle C downward, may *temporarily shut down*, and its tones become inaccessible to the singer. In that case, she should stop performing the exercises, completely rest her voice for a day or two, then upon returning to the exercise session, *do not employ the i (ee) vowel at all*, but instead employ the AW or the a (ah) vowel to single, individually sustained tones, singing them softly, then, when it feels appropriate, swelling the selected tone to a *f* dynamic, then returning it to the original *p* dynamic. Then the singer may return to the open, detached falsetto i (ee) vowel version of these exercises.

Descending, "detached falsetto" exercises selected from the Top Range

Below are three sets of descending scale exercises, employing the *"detached falsetto"* voice, which should be executed very slowly, paying strict attention to the *legato application. The keys of these exercises should be raised and lowered, in order to encompass as much of the complete range, with the muscular controls of the upper register. If the singer experiences difficulty in accessing the extremely soft "top" tones, she should pass on to the descending scales that start with E2 and with them, gradually descend to the Bottom Range. This does not mean that there is anything wrong with not being able to access the higher, soft tones, but rather that the individual's voice is responding in its own way to this vocal structuring exercise, and this must be respected.*

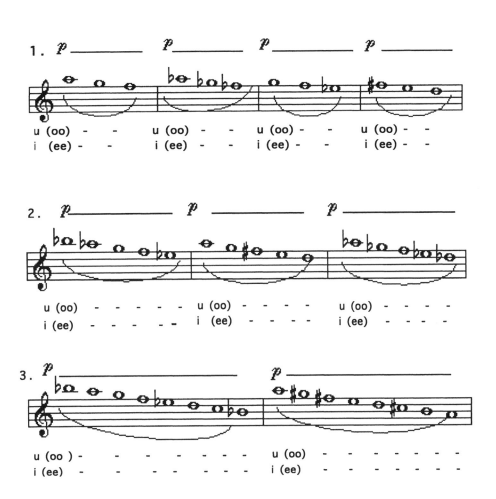

Until all *"detached falsetto controlled"* tones from E2 downward to middle C have been strengthened to the point that they are capable of bringing in to play the desired "core brilliance" of the chest voice, it is not critical to perform a great many exercises with the tones from F2 upward, *to the highest point of potential development.* However, there are exceptions to this rule. While striving to develop the tones from E2 downward to Middle C, the singer must periodically put that work aside and perform exercises with the higher tones, from F2 upward, where the fullest flow of the breath force and the purest form of vocal "purity" may always be accessed. Vowel purity, obtained in that range area, represents the standard of "purity", that should be applied to all the developing tones from E2 downward to Middle C, endeavoring to prevent them from becoming *"bottom heavy"*, due to the negative influences of the lower register. To begin the process of making the two registers harmonic with each other, the singer must carry the qualities and muscular controls of the upper register, along with a free flow of breath *(accessed in the very Top Range)*, far downward in the range to the lower registers' break, then below it.

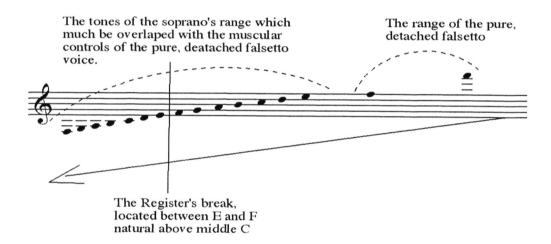

The tones of the soprano's range which much be overlaped with the muscular controls of the pure, deatached falsetto voice.

The range of the pure, detached falsetto

The Register's break, located between E and F natural above middle C

The unusual lower octave of all correctly structured singing voices

Most singers are unaware of the unusual nature and functions of the lower octave, *after all* its tones have been properly restructured to match the upper octave. Traditionally, ascending scales are naively applied to the lower octave's tones with the intention of creating tonal *"solidity"*, and *"extending"* the singer's range upward. Instead of granting positive results, these ascending scales *negatively add weight and thickness to the lower octave*, which it time proves destructive. But *not all* ascending scales produce negative effects upon the singing voice. In many instances they are vitally needed, in order to create an *"open throated"* pathway from the bottom of the range to its top. Ascending scales using properly *"blended"* tones, tones that have been *"mixed"* with the *head voice's muscular helpful influences*, are useful. Performing an ascending scale *without* this critical *"mixed voice"* factor forces the muscular controls of the single, lower register to sustaining the complete *"work load"* of the ascent, solely on it own. An ascending scale, operating *solely* with the muscular controls of the lower register, can only ascend to the pitch of E2, the top note of the *Middle Range.* Above that point, the scale *can not* ascend further upward without radical forcing. This leaves the Bottom Range undeveloped, with breathy, unstable tones of inferior quality and poor control.

"Classical Singing" is an art form in which *anything less than near-perfect will not suffice.* The path of vocal history is strewn with singers, possessing superior voices, who seemingly advance rapidly in the profession, then suddenly fall back downward into oblivion, due to faulty, incomplete vocal structuring. Singers must learn that, unlike all other musical instruments, the singing voice has a capricious, unstable aspect to its behavior. But, sound structuring principles make allowances for the many unexpected, whimsical changes that the singing voice undergoes *throughout a professional career.*

When performing an ascending scale, employing a *"team effort"* of both registers' muscular controls allows the singer to correctly manage the *"work load"* of the ascending scale, which, in order to be correctly accomplished, demands a gradual increase of breath tension, to accomplish each successive higher pitch. The singer who can successfully ascend through *the lower octave of her range, with beauty of tone and pure vowels,* and arrive at the upper octave of her range without being dissuaded by *the cumbersome, negative weight and thickness* of the lower register, is truly remarkably talented.

Prior to correct structuring, the upper register's vitally necessary, muscular controls are *inoperative in the lower octave.* However, they must be *"installed"* there, through repeated applications of descending falsetto scales. Once this has been accomplished, the advanced, developed upper register manifests an *upward pulling motion,* by pulling upward and away from the power of the lower register. This is especially so, when singing a correctly produced, *open i (ee) vowel. This "upward pulling action"* serves an important purpose. It aids the singer to smoothly accomplish all ascending scales, *in a similar manner of the gliding steps of an escalator.*

When singing correctly, the developed *upper register pulls upward and away from the power of the lower register,* while *the lower register pull downwards, in the opposite direction.* This lower register's downward pulling is also *correct and necessary.* The singer utilizes it to counter the *upward pull* of the upper register. These *upward and downward pulls* are the only manner by which the singer can control the ascending and descending movements of her singing voice. This unexpected behavioral pattern of the two separate registers, after their inherent antagonism toward each other has been eliminated, graphically illustration how all inherent, *"negative energy"* can be *converted* into *"positive energy".* The objective of the exercises in

Figures 1, 2, and 3 (below) are to transport the purest muscular actions and qualities of the upper-middle area, downward in the range. The detached falsetto *u (oo)* and i *(ee) vowels* are useful for achieving that purpose. It is acceptable to experiment with the remaining three vowels.

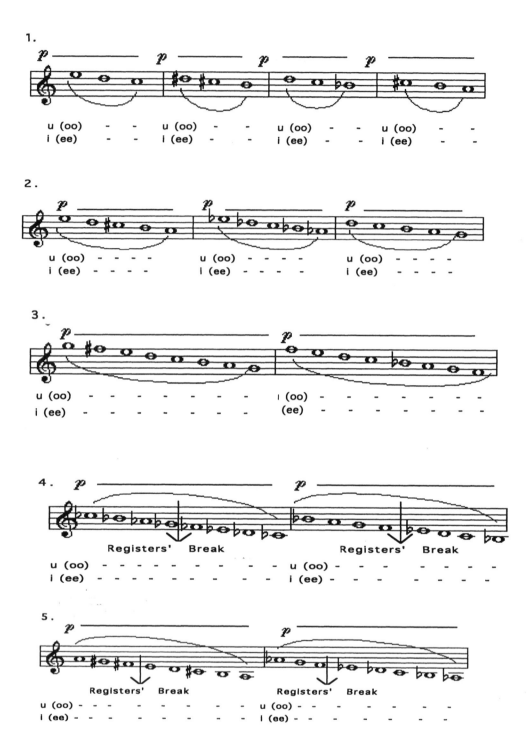

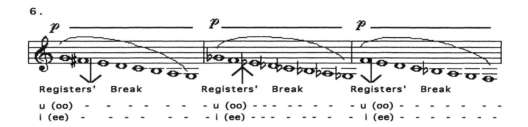

6.

Registers' Break   Registers' Break   Registers' Break

u (oo) - - - - - - - u (oo) - - - - - - - - u (oo) - - - - - - - -
i (ee) - - - - - - i (ee) - - - - - - - i (ee) - - - - - - - -

The *exercises* of *Figures 4, 5, and 6* descend towards, and cross through the r*egisters' break,* located between E♮ and F♮ *above* middle C, then they descend further to the low F♮ *below* middle C, thereby embracing all of the soprano's Lower Range *"chest tones"*.

The singer will find the *u (oo)* and i *(ee) vowels* very compatible, but their purest forms are difficult to produce in the lower range. However, these descending *u (oo) and i (ee)* vowel scales will be most welcomed by the extreme lower tones, since they help *"narrow"* and *"thin in"* them away from their inherent, undesirable *"bulk"* factor .

Matching all developing tones to the highest tone of the upper register

As the muscles that control *the detached-falsetto tones* of the upper register progressively develop strength, they eventually *"invite"* the vibrato action of the lower register to join them. After an extended period of training, the qualities of both registers come to *"match"* each other *(sound wise),* and they fully collaborate with each other. But at that advanced stage, when so many exchanges of both registers have occurred, it often becomes difficult for the singer to distinguish and identify the separate individual muscular actions and sounds of each respective register, in their newly transformed state.

One infallible method of making clear distinctions between the two registers is for the singer to understand that *all head registers tones (when disconnected form the chest register)* posses an ample flow of the breath stream. And conversely, *all chest voice tones (when disconnected from the heard voice),* possess *no air flow at all,* in their production. When the singer connects the muscular actions of the two registers together, the air flow has to make an adjustment to the power that's been joined to the starter falsetto tone. This manifest itself by a narrowing and focusing of the breath flow's stream, and a shrinking of throat-socket of the vowel that is presently being sung, to a smaller aperture. But the singer must never let this vowel's narrowing throat-socket close completely, otherwise that would stop the breath flow, and the tone being sung.

Another important principle to keep it mind is that, all developing tones should be matched in quality *to the highest tone of the singer's Top Range, not to the Bottom Range.* During each "warm up" session, when the singer is preparing the *"slumbering"* voice for singing, her first tones must *be started with the purest, softest detached-falsetto tone,* using the u (oo), o (oh), or the AW vowel, which enables the breath to flow freely. The AW vowel is a composite of the u (oo), o (oh) and a (ah) vowels. It is only *after having establish a detached falsetto tone*, with any of the above mentioned vowels, that the singer may swell the starter tone, in order to bring into play the *vibrato action* and "power" of the lower register to join the tone.

All the principles presented thus far are meant to guide the reader through the many possible structural discoveries which result from applying the *"Head Voice Training System"*. This method is seldom understood, has presently fallen out of use, and it is often highly distrusted. Its principles are painstakingly slow to accomplish. And, in view of the first tonal sounds which the beginner is likely to produce with it, it will give her little confidence that it is the correct approach to vocal training. For these reasons, it is very easy to understand how the damaging *"Chest Voice Training System" which is more aurally tangible, and less complex, and to which the voice seems to respond rather quickly*, has gained such widespread popularity.

Here are some interesting things which some extremely talented singers had said about the *passaggio:*

Luciano Pavarotti: *"Now this passaggio . . . "*

Jerome Hinds: *(cutting in on Pavarotti) " . . . is the transition from the upper middle voice to the high voice, and I know that students are interested in your approach, since you have a flawless passaggio; it is so smooth a change, one is not aware of it".*

Luciano Pavarotti: *"It took me six years of study, and one must be convinced of its importance from the first day . . . never change ideas. You know, the first five or six months it is very depressing because it does not come out right, and you become cyanotic, red in the face. Then the student begins to think this approach is wrong, and tries the other way, but it will never bring them security of voice.*

Luciano Pavarotti -   Great Singers on Singing / Jerome Hinds

None of the exercises presented in this manual should be considered less important than any other, nor considered to be of "transitory use". They are the permanent tools which efficiently and correctly establish and maintain superior vocal usage, and the health for the singer's entire vocal lifetime.

CHAPTER FIVE

The messa di voce —A brief history of the exercise

The *messa di voce* exercise is one of the oldest and most useful exercises available to contemporary singers for structuring a superior singing instrument. It was created by the master singer-teachers of the *Scuola Cantorum,* a musical conservatory assigned by Pope Sylvester *(314-336 A.D.),* to fully investigate all technical matters regarding singing, and the singing instrument. This investigation ultimately fostered the age of the *castrati (castrated male singers). During this period, female voices were not considered, since in 1856 Pope Urban had issued a Papal Declaration in that no female voices be used in the services of the church*; also forbidden were *non castrated males,* tenors, baritones and basses. These vocal categories emerged much later, in the late 18th and early 19th centuries.

The great value of the *messa di voce* exercise was generally recognized from the time of the *Scuola Cantorum,* and the exercise continued to find favor throughout many subsequent important vocal periods. It was greatly relied upon by the teachers of the *Bel Canto* era, and the *"Golden Age of Song",* which flourished in Italy during the post-Renaissance period. During the former period, the art of singing is acknowledged to have achieved its highest degree of perfection.

The exercise remained vitally important through the late 17th and early 18th centuries, into the time of such prodigious singer-teachers as *Manual Garcia I (Père)* and his son *Manual Garcia II (Patricio Rodriguez).* The exercise was also very popular during the colorful Paris vocal period of the late 18th and early 19th centuries; a *"glamorous" and "colorful"* period dominated by the flamboyant tenor, *Jean de Reszke.* Then the exercise's popularity began to wane. In America, it was almost totally discarded in or about the 1950's.

However, more recently, it was displayed through the superior singing of *Milanov, Tebaldi, Callas, Sutherland, Scotto, and Caballé.* This seems absurd, since a serious scholar may go to any reliable library and find documentation confirming that the *messa di voce* exercise was considered to be an invaluable training tool by most teachers of the *"great vocal past".* Why, then, has this exercise been discarded by modern singers and teachers?

By its basic nature, *"the messa di voce's principle of swelling and diminishing"* a selected tone, all superior training methods must utilize this exercise. The most significant reason why the *messa di voce* exercise has fallen into disuse is that, with contemporary singers, even the most patient and diligent application of its principles meets with predictable failure. The mandate of the exercise is that the singer start an tone with the softest volume, swell it to the intensity of a *forte,* then return the tone, without taking a new breath, back once again to the original *pianissimo.*

This feat can hardly be accomplished by most of today's professional singers, with the exception of the *lightest and highest coloratura sopranos* and *leggero* tenors, much less by beginning students. The question then arises: In what ways were the great teachers of the historical past able to successfully use the *messa di voce* exercise?

These voice teachers of the historical past were applying the exercise exclusively to the voices of the *castrati* singers, or more plainly said, *castrated men*. Because of castration, these *"male-sopranos"* vocal mechanisms became permanently altered, resulting in denial of the full muscular growth of their *lower register's muscles*. Consequently, *their upper register's muscles became dominant.* As a consequence, when *castrati* performed the *messa di voce* exercise, *they did so with upper register muscles that were different from non castrated men.* Therefore, the *castrati's head voice muscles* could *more readily* swell the selected tone to the point where the lower register's action could be added to it, than could a non castrated man. Because the inherent power of the *castrati's* lower register muscles was nullified, through castration, these *castrati* could facilely *"pull up"* whatever vibrato action of the lower register's muscular controls remained *after castration*. Thus, they could achieve completely "blended" tones, *(through the use of the messa di voce),* which possessed the tonal attributes and muscular controls of *both the chest and head registers*. And they could successfully make harmonic, the separate, antagonistic muscular actions of the two registers into a collaboratory *"team"* which is almost impossible for contemporary singers, including females.

Where the *messa di voce exercise and* contemporary females singers are concerned, contrary to the *castrati* of the past, who gained many advantages through their castration, most contemporary female students set up a vocal training system that creates a great disadvantage for themselves, by completely abandoning the use of the chest register. They do so, by complaining that the *chest register* is too *"thick"*, *"weighty"*, *"bulky"* and *"unmusical"* to add to their *"lighter"*, *"thinner"*, *"more musical"* and *"easily managed"* head voice register. Once that decision has been made, there is no reason for female singers to employ the *messa di voce, at all. Recall that, the ultimate accomplishment of the messa di voce is to unite the <u>two vocal</u> register.* Therefore, after abandoning the chest voice's help, present-day female singers *employ but one, single vocal register, instead of the two registers required to create a superior voice. And so, a major factor becomes missing from their training procedures which make the use of the messa di voce improbable.*

As long as contemporary female singers assume that they can get by without the *chest voice's help,* while singing, a tragic voice training scenario will be played out, over and over:

A young female vocal student who originally possesses a beautifully clear, undamaged range of head voice tones, begins taking voice lessons. Her *"head voice"* tones grow rapidly and her singing is commendable, and seemingly effortless. She and her associates—*her teacher, her parents, her vocal coach*—encourage her to make plans to enjoy a professional career. She gets by for a year or so, perhaps even more, without the help of her *chest voice*, and without addressing the critical issue of the synergistic needs of both her vocal registers. Then suddenly, unexpectedly, her voice *"shuts completely down!"* Questions and doubts arise: maybe she has *over sung?* Maybe *she's tired?* She should rest her voice? She does so, then tries her voice again, but the *"old facile, lovely singing voice"* will not respond, as it once did. What should she do? *The answer—find a reliable voice teacher who knows a great deal about the synergistic needs of the two vocal registers and immediately start studying with him/her!*

Exercise No. 3 Contemporary applications of the mess di voce exercise

The *"dramatic"* nature of much contemporary vocal literature demands that singers, of all vocal categories, employ a greater percentage of "chest voice" musculature, than singers of earlier times. As a result, the voices of contemporary singers performing that strenuous material, eventually grow progressively "larger" and "bulkier" with use. This makes their voices strongly resistant to the *messa di voce* exercise, and has caused the exercise to seem totally inapplicable to contemporary vocal training.

This misconception can be rectified by presenting some modified ways in which the *messa di voce* can be successfully applied. With the presentation of *Exercise No. 3*, the time has come to apply *breath pressure intensity, in incrementally increased amounts, to a selected tone (s), to develop its muscular strength.*

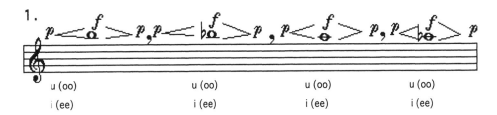

Figure 1 presents several *messa di voce exercises. Note that these* tones are presented in a *descending direction.* They should be performed, individually, and in that same direction, and with a purest, detached head voice tone, meaning that the selected tone starts out with no connection what-so-ever to the power of the chest voice. This purity is meant to preserve as much upper registers muscular dominance, and purity of tone and vowel as is possible.

The "note filate exercise" — a compromised version of the messa di voce

The old master-teachers, of the post *bel canto* period of voice training knew how difficult it was for any singer to achieve a perfect *messa di voce,* with all the tones of her range. So, they made allowances for *temporary failure* by creating another, *"compromised"* version of the *ideal messa di voce.* It was called the *note filate* exercise. When a singer had reached the midway point of the swelling process, from a *pp dynamic start, to a f* dynamic, and she sensed that it was not possible to advance the swelling of the tone further, nor diminish it back to the soft *p* intensity, she was allowed to *"cut off"* the tone, take a new breath, quickly re-attack the tone with the *f* dynamic, then make a new effort to either swell the tone further, or gradually diminish it's volume back to the soft *p* intensity, thereby successfully completing a *note filate* exercise, which is *a compromised version of the messa di voce.* When the *note filate* became nearly perfect it was put aside. The singer could then perform an *ideal* rendition of the more challenging *messa di voce* exercise. The principles of the *note filate* exercise may be used by contemporary sopranos, too.

If the singer feels that the pitches of *Figures #1 (abovc),* are uncomfortably high, she may perform her *messa di voce* exercise with these lower pitches: *E♮2, E♭2, D♮2, D♭2, or a C♮2.*

To execute the pitches of *Figs. 1,* the singer should start the tone with a *pp* intensity, swell the tone to a potential volume of *f,* then return to the starting *p* intensity. The singer is urged to take brief rest periods between exercises. However, she is at liberty to perform the exercises for perhaps one and a half hour a day, eventually increasing the swelling process of the tone to a louder intensity of say *ff,* provided there are some quarter or half hour rest breaks. At this stage, complete success with the exercise is *not* expected.

While attempting the *messa di voce, there* may occur one of two *"breaks"* or *"crackings apart"* of the two registers. Don't be alarmed. A common misconception is that this undesirable breaking apart of the two registers occurs only at a single, specific point in the vocal range—usually between E♮ and F♮ above middle C. While most "breakings apart" of the registers do occur in that rage area, the potential for "breaking" and/or "cracking" a tone exists with any tone. Understand and take comfort that, it is only when the attempt to joint the *two registers* fails that that a potential for this "breaking" factor may occur, not when *but only one register is* being evoked. Besides, the single register tone can never become a proper permanent, superior tone, no matter how deceptively *"good"* and *"comfortable"* it feels, when producing it. When practicing the *messa di voce exercise, as* difficult as it is to control the separate, antagonistic muscular actions of both registers, at the point of the registers' break, with much patience, time, and seemingly endless applications of the exercise, that feat is highly attainable

Another reason why so many contemporary attempts at the *messa di voce* fail is because the *starter-tone* if frequently *"impure"!* Meaning, the tone's purity is corrupted by some element of the undesirable chest voice. A *truly pure head voice, starter-tone* must be selected from the Top Range, F2♮ to the B2♮ above it, where the breath flow swirls about in the sinuses and head cavities at their *"strongest, wildest and freest."* Any tone selected outside of this area of the range, within either the *Middle Range* or the *Bottom Range* must begin with a starter-tone that possess as strong "swirling currents of breath" in it, as a tone selected from the *Top Range.*

It should be obvious that an ideal starter-tone for the *messa di voce* exercise must be modeled on the sounds and physical sensations that occur with the pitches of the Top Range, and totally free from all vocal cords' vibrations and connections to the chest voice, and *totally free* from all *"throat sensations".* When operating successfully, the tone's mode of behavior must be akin to a ping-pong ball, being tossed about on the top of a fountain-spray. If the fountain's spray is too strong, it will toss the ball off the water spray and into the air, away from the fountain. If it the fountain's spray is too weak, the ball will roll off the top of the fountain spray and fall into the fountain below.

Do not expect quick results with your first attempts of the *messa di voce. Merely keep focusing on its ultimate goal, which is to eliminate the "separateness" of muscular actions between the chest and head voice.* Presently, only the lightest coloratura sopranos seem able to perform the exercise, to near exacting standards. Even so, they can only succeed with but a very few tones. at the top of their ranges. Presently, most large-voice singers cannot perform even one correct version of the exercise. Some tones of a heavy-voiced singer's *"break area"* take many years to perfect. One should *not* be discouraged by this, since, by performing the *"compromised version"* of the exercise, over a long period of time, it grants many benefits, along the way, until total success with the *messa di voce is* accomplished. The most important of these benefits is that, *partial success* they gradually erode the *negative bulk and weight* of the Lower Register.

Solving the structural needs of the *passaggio's tones* has been a problematic mystery for singers of all vocal categories, throughout all past periods of vocal training. For example, *Emma Calvé (1858-1942),* who had originally been a star pupil of *Matilde Marchesi (1821-1913),* from whom she learned all about her *"fourth voice",* her high register's *"whistle voice",* later on had to study approximately seven years with the great *castrato Domenico Mustafà (1829-1912),* to successfully structure her *"lower break's"* tones.

By infusing all your *Bottom Range's* tones with great amount of *breath flow,* and, rendering them *"hollow"* through descending scale applications of the *u (oo), and o (oh),* and *AW vowels,* will greatly help the singer to eventually succeed with the *messa di voce exercise.*

It is seldom understood that strengthening the upper register's detached falsetto muscles, or *"the whistle voice",* with the *messa di voce,* permanently effects a major, positive change to all the tones of the *Middle and Lower Range.*

The Resonance Channel—or as the Italians called it —"The colona sonora"

The primary benefit which contemporary singers may derive from the *"updated"* applications of the *messa di voce exercise,* is to begin the transformation of the upper section of the *"vocal tract."* It is at the bottom end of this *resonance channel* that the *breath force's sound waves,* emanating from the vocal cords, travel upward and posteriorly, then into the various resonance cavities: the *mouth pharynx cavity,* then further upward into the *cavities of the sinuses and the skull, and all of these resonance cavities exert an enormous influence upon the singing voice.* And so, the singer begins creating the resonance channel, from *top—to—bottom, not* from *bottom—to—top!* Using, first, the experiences gained at the *Top Range,* as a model for structuring the Bottom Range. This is the only way to insure a correctly structured singing instrument that can meet all the demands of ideal singing, and withstand the "wear and tear" of so much frequent use.

"Source" and "Resonator"

The successful playing of all musical instruments requires a mandatory dual-coupling system. This represents a scientific law, in which *"the source", or originator of the sound— Factor #1*, must be coupled with a corresponding resonator—*Factor #2. The violin,* whose strings, *"the* source", generate the original vibrations of the instrument—*Factor #1*, must couple with the *terminal resonator points* inside the wooden chamber of the instrument, the "resonator"—*Factor #2. The trumpet,* whose mouth piece, along with the trumpeter's lips, serves as *"the source"* or the generators of the instrument pitches— *Factor #1*, must be coupled with *the terminal points for each pitch*, along the passageway of the main body of the instrument, *"the resonator"—Factor #2.*

This *"dual-coupling-system"* law is also mandatory for the *Singing Instrument.* Therefore, the *vocal cords—Factor #1*, which produces the original vibrations of all pitches, *"the source"* must couple with—*Factor #2*, the resonance cavities, located in various areas along the length of the *resonance channe*l, and situated far above the vocal cords, while, the muscles of the vocal registers—*Factor #2,* which enable the singer to couple it with *Factor #1,* are in a state of antagonism, until after restructuring. Therefore, it is critical for all singers to bring the two antagonistic registers into complete harmony with each other. If the singer fails to do so, she can not enable her vocal instrument to obey the mandatory dual coupling law, which is required of all musical instruments.

Through a successful performance of the *messa di voce exercise,* the barrier which exists in the *mid-section* of the resonance channel, and which inherently *"blocks"* the vocal cords' vibrations from flowing freely upward in the range on the breath flow, and into resonance cavities, can be removed. This *"blockage"* of the resonance channel *is the tongue.* This is so because the tongue consistently positions itself disadvantageously to the singer purpose of *"uniting"* the vibrations of the vocal cords, which emanate from the lower throat channel, with these appropriate "resonance cavities" located far above the lower channel, in the upper middle or top of the resonance channel. While another *"blockage factor",* the soft palate, when wrongly positioned, blocks the rising breath flow. While actually singing, to remove this blockage, the tongue must be *re*positioned in the mouth cavity, *through special exercises,* and its center section made to form a mound, which mimics the shape of the hard palate, above it, while the tongue's tip must be placed below the lower front teeth.

The soft palate, in its usual position, tends to rise upward and backward in the upper posterior part of the mouth-pharynx cavity, *the area where we gargle,* positions itself there horizontally, and blocks the air flow, upon which the vocal cords' vibrations travel. The soft palate must be moved downward and forward, *with the help of the detached falsetto, open i (ee) vowel,* in order to allow the breath flow, transporting the vocal cords' vibrations, to travel *behind it,* then *upward* and *into the resonance cavities of the sinus and skull.*

I have dealt extensively with both the tongue and soft palate training and positioning in my latest vocal manual entitled, The Art of Singing on the Breath Flow, which may be purchased at Patelsen's Music House, 160 West 56th street, Manhattan, NY, Zip-10019, Tel: (212) 757-5587.

The thickness/thinness adjustments of the vocal cords

Accurate vocal pitches are the product of *the vocal cords* having an *exact length and width,* adjusted by one of the five classic vowels, and a specific amount of breath pressure being applied to a selected pitch. Every tone of the singer's range is also produced by a slightly different laryngeal-pharyngeal adjustment. There are many gradations of the *vibrator mass.* In other words, different lengths and thicknesses of the vocal cords are engaged, and different proportions of the *chest or head voice's muscular contributions* to a selected tone, to fulfill each individual pitch. When ascending the range increased amount of breath pressure must be applied against the vocal cords, and they become gradually shorter and thinner. Conversely, *when descending the range* they lengthen and thicken. This demands "exact tension", which must be understood to be *"breath tension",* in the form of a focused stream energy,

A strong, driving breath-force is created by the build-up of pressure in the lungs, in response to the singer purposefully *"holding back all the inspired air"* within her lungs. When this breath-tension is focused against the vocal cords, they yield to it with a *bowing action.* The vocal cords first open in a rapid-fire movement, allowing some of the energized breath tension to escape through them, in the form of an energized puff of breath, then they rapidly close, whereupon a new cycle of the same exact behavior is initiated. In other word, the vocal cords come together, separate, come together again, then separate again.

This cycle continues as long as a musical note is being prolonged. For the singer to raise the pitch, the amount of breath-force being applied to the vocal cords must be proportionately *increased.* When descending the scale, the breath tension must be proportionately *decreased.* Even a beginning singer has relatively easy access to the varying amounts of breath tension that must be applied to the vocal cords. *But, she has no direct control over the adjustments of the vocal cords, where precise length* and *thickness* are required.

The illustration *below* shows an *incorrect* vocal condition, with a *"disconnected",* "broken", and "dysfunctional" resonance channel, which creates a wrong pathway, that the vibrations of the vocal cords, and the energized breath stream are forced to take, into the mouth cavity, then out of it, over the lower front teeth, *instead of the correct pathway upward* and backward behind the soft palate. This wrong pathway is unavoidably taken by those singers whose registers' break area *has not* been properly restructured to facilitate the rising breath flow, along its proper pathway.

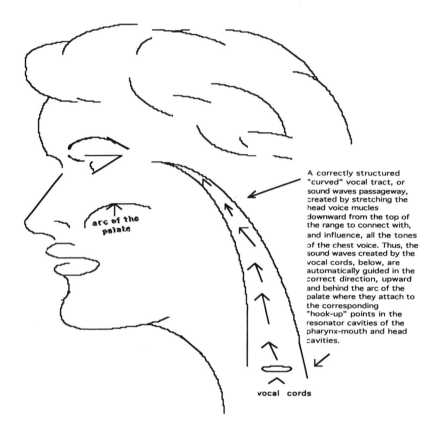

arc of the palate

A correctly structured "curved" vocal tract, or sound waves passageway, created by stretching the head voice mucles downward from the top of the range to connect with, and influence, all the tones of the chest voice. Thus, the sound waves created by the vocal cords, below, are automatically guided in the correct direction, upward and behind the arc of the palate where they attach to the corresponding "hook-up" points in the resonator cavities of the pharynx-mouth and head cavities.

vocal cords

Now, compare the incorrect illustration *(on the previous page),* with the *correct illustration above.* In this case, the resonance channel is properly positioned and the breath stream, mixed with the vibrations of the vocal cords, has been properly directed by the singer along the correct pathway leading upward from the vocal cords, then backward, behind the arc of the soft and hard palates, into the resonator cavities of the posterior area of the pharynx-mouth, then further up the resonance channel, to the cavities of the sinuses and skull, to attach themselves to their appropriate *"hook-up"* points.

Increases and decreases of the vibratory mass

When an ascending scale is precisely executed, incremental *decreases* in the vibratory mass occur. In other words, with each successive higher note, the vocal cords undergo a "shortening/thickening" adjustment, with regard to their relative position to each other. This, in turn, causes a gradual elimination of the *vibratory mass.* At the *bottom of the singer's range*, the tones are produces with a "longer/thicker" vocal cords adjustment. At the *top of the range*, the tones are produced with a "shorter/thinner" vocal cord adjustment. This is correct and desirable. There are those who believe that accomplishing the *shortening-or-lengthening, thinning-or-thickening process* of the vocal cords is simply a matter of discovering the right "aesthetic concept" of singing. Every singing student quickly realizes that without proper structuring of her complete singing range, whenever she is assigned an ascending scale, she can only produce an unmusical, unwieldy one which becomes *louder* and *uglier* as it rises, and *exhibits no musicality or vowel purity.*

The Top Range

Now, let's examine the physiological nature of *each individual section* of the complete *resonance channel*, with further regard to *"the thickening and thinning process."* At the upper area of the resonance channel, or the *"Top Ran~* 　e cavities of the sinuses and skull are located. These resonance cavities are *smaller in si~* 　　　'ections of the complete resonance channel. When the singers accesses a selected 　　　　e's borders— F♮2 to the B♮2,

~ thinnest and shortest adjustments thin the borders of the two other, ~, when the *breath flow(the* 'is *Top Range's* resonance ~ance cavities, compresses intense stream; *much* ~perating in any other

l 　　　　　　　　　　　　　　　　　　　　'*concepts, but rather actual physical factors which*
s~ 　　　　　　　　　　　　　　　　　　*~ratory mass" of all the tones located within the*
res~
helps 　　　　　　　　　　　　　　　　*~ne illustration above, how small the opening of the*
borde~ 　　　　　　　　　　　　　*~Middle Range or the Bottom Range.*
glottis i.

Th~ ~~te Range

The mouth-pharynx cavity is located in the *middle area of the complete resonance channel.* It houses the *"upper passaggio"* of all female singers. The mouth-pharynx cavity is *medium sized.* A the mouth-pharynx's upper, posterior area, the soft palate is situated, and it is situated the entrance to *the resonance cavities of sinuses and the skull* of the *Top Range.*

The mouth-pharynx cavity, or *passaggio,* is *domed shaped,* and it is larger than the Top Range's resonance cavities, by compassion. It is also very differently shaped than the cavities of the Top Range, and that of the windpipe's cavity, situated at the very Bottom Range, which is longer and wider than the two resonance cavities, situated above it.

When the singers directs the intensified *breath stream* into *mouth-pharynx cavity,* its swirling currents behave differently there, than when in all other areas of the resonance channel. The mouth-pharynx cavity houses the legendary and mysterious *"mixed tones",* which are made up of currents of cool air that mix, *but only at the singer urgings,* with the vibrations of the vocal cords.

All five halftones of the Middle Range, C♮2, C♯2, D♮2, D♯2, E♮2 are frequently the most abused tones of the complete range, since most singers *mistakenly think of them as the top of the lower range,* consequently, they force these pitches to an *", destructive width",* in a vain effort to match them to the *Bottom Range's* width. Whereas, they should all be matched to the thinner, detached *falsetto i (ee) vowel's*

muscular contours of the Top Range's tones, and muscularly made to be *"head voice"* dominated. The tones of mouth-pharynx cavity are the most difficult to understand and structure. When the singer properly accesses a selected pitch located within Middle Range's resonance cavity, the vocal cords adjust themselves to a *medium sized,* narrow, vertical slit. This opening of the glottis assumes a much larger, longer, and wider position there, than when the singer sings a tone located within the Top Range. *(See the aboves illustration of the vocal cords, when they are operating in the Middle Range.)*

To produce the tones of the *Middle Range, with superior tone and pure vowels,* demands the utmost skill of the singer. If these *"capricious"* tones are not individually produce with *"mixed"* and *"precise amounts"* of the breath flow and vibrations of the vocal cords, they will *bog down with excessive chest voice weight and thicken, so that,* when the singer tries to sing a higher tone, located within the *Top Range, the* accumulated negative *chest weight and thickness* in the *Middle Range* will deny her attempt to ascend upward and out of the *Middle Range.* And, at another time, these middle tones may disconnect themselves totally from the power of the chest voice, and leave empty spots in the Middle Range, which are totally useless to the singer.

There exist other *critical problems* which the singer encounters, while singing the tones of the *Middle Range,* and they are most often due to the wrong positioning and behavior of both *the tongue* and the *soft palate.*

The tongue generally lies loosely in the lower throat channel and *blocks* the *air flow* from entering into the mouth pharynx cavity, then passing, as is desired, above it, and into the cavities of the sinuses and the skull. To solve this problem, the singer must raise her tongue upward and out of the lower throat channel, and place it into her mouth-pharynx cavity. Once it is there, the tongue's center section must rise upward toward the hard palate and form *a mound,* while the tip of the tongue must be moved forward and positioned behind the lower front teeth. At the same time, the *soft palate* must be moved downward and forward, towards the front of the mouth cavity. Accomplishing all the above will close off the mouth cavity, and redirect the air from flow upward behind the soft and hard palates, then further upward, in to the cavities of the sinuses and skull, when the singer intends to sing her Top Range's tones.

These structural rearrangements of the tongue and soft palate's positions and behavior can only be accomplished by the use of *the detached falsetto, open i (ee) vowel,* with pitches selected from her Top Range, and applied in a descending direction, tone by tone, first to the tones located above *Upper Break* area: G♮, G♭, F♯, E♮, E♭, D♮, D♭—*above C♯2*—then afterwards, the same exact pitches, but an octave lower, in the "true" Lower Break area.

A detached, falsetto, open i (ee) vowel is one that has been "threaded through" the vowel-throat-space of a silent, open-throated a (ah) vowel. All these above factors are purely mechanical factors, and not merely mental concepts. They accomplish "the reduction of the vibratory mass", of all the tones of the Middle Range, and make an open, free passageway for the energized breath stream to travel upward and downward along it.

There are other difficulties that are frequently experienced with the Middle Range's tones. For one, all "pronunciation" of language that accompanies all vocal music, occurs within the *Middle Range's* borders. By *"pronunciation" we mean something entirely different* than when speaking; something that is more akin to what a ventriloquist does, when attempting to make his dummy partner, sound like he's doing the actual talking.

Relative to the above, we mean that while singing, the tongue's movement becomes greatly restricted in range, in order to accomplish the clear and accurate *"pronunciation"* of the words of a song, or an operatic aria. For example, while singing with a superior structured voice, the tip of the tongue accomplishes all clear, readily understood *"vocal pronunciation", not the entire tongue.* And, the consonants are managed by the upper lip, with little or no help from the lower lip. The task of *superior singing* focuses 99% of the time on establishing the *"vowel of the moment"*, operating in the rear, upper area of the throat, and it spends the least amount of time, only *1%, on accomplishing the pronunciation of the consonants.*

All these above, mechanical factors facilitate the mechanical ways in which the vocal instrument operates, in order to accommodate the "reduction of the vibratory mass" of all tones.

The Bottom Range

When correctly structured, the Bottom Range generally produces "dark", "sonorous", "wide open, resonant sounds" that create the greatest of illusions for the singer's listeners, as to how they are actually muscularly produced, *when compared to all the other tones of the complete singing range.* These greatly misunderstood *"dark, sonorous, wide-open, resonant sounds"* of the bottom range occur, due to the fact that the *bottom section of resonance channel* is situated closest, of all sections of the resonance channel to the *"voice box"*, which contain the vocal cords. And, the vocal cords, at the *bottom section of the complete range are said to vibrate in their entire length and thickest width.* It is this factor, the middle range's tones being located so close to the vocal cords, which produces these unusual vocal sounds, which are so extremely difficult to understand.

When the singer directs the *breath stream* toward a particular pitch located within the *lowest resonance cavity,* this particular resonance cavity's unusual shape, which is tubular, longer and wider than the resonance cavities of the mouth-pharynx, sinus cavities and head cavities, and somewhat like a section of the clarinet, the glottis assumes their widest opening. It is this widest opening position of the vocal cords, and the full force of the breath stream, blasting open the glottis, then rushing upward along the resonance channel, on its way to one of the higher resonance cavities, that creates these deceptive *"dark, sonorous, wide-open, resonant, sounds"* in the singer's lower range of the voice. This lowest resonance cavity also gives the singer's listeners the impression that the singer's lowest tones are "solid" and "steel-like" in structure, when in fact they are merely "strong, pulsing currents of breath", mixing with the *vibrations of the vocal cords,* which are physically situated so close to this lower resonance cavity. But in fact, the tones of this lowest resonance cavity must be thought of, by the singer, as the least solid of all the tones of her complete range, otherwise they *will not* allow the singer to sing her *Middle and Top range tones accurately.* Perhaps the airiness of these lowest tones can be better understood by relating them to the "dark" and "heavy" sounds that result, when one blows the breath stream into a large, empty jug, creating *Aeolian* sounds.

When the singer directs the breath stream into the Bottom Range, frequently referred to as the "chest voice", *this shallow section* of the *resonance channel, which is the least effective, of all the singing voice's resonance chambers, merely <u>re</u>sounds, colors, and amplifies* the original vibrations of the vocal cords, causing their *actual* method of tone production to be easily misinterpreted.

Correctly adding the *power factor* to any of these Bottom Range's tones can only be accomplished if *the entire length of Bottom Range's resonance cavity has been brought to a state of complete emptiness, or hollowness.* This is accomplished by blowing the Aeolian breath stream into them, tone by tone, employing a descending scale pattern and the hollow u (oo), o (oh) or AW vowels, while temporarily "holding out" all "core" vibrations, until the singer knows clearly how to accomplish that task.

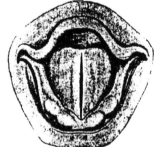

The "hollowing out" of this lowest resonance cavity, with the "hollow" u (oo) and o (oh) vowels, must be done for quite a long time, while at the same time, the tones from C2 upward in the range, to it very top, are being given structural preference, sometimes using the detached falsetto, open i (ee) or e (eh) vowels. Much later, all these Bottom Range tones must have the core brilliant added back into them, by performing single-tone, sustained exercises that employ the u (oo), o (oh), then gradually changing the throat-sockets of the u (oo) and/or o (oh), vowels to an open i (ee) vowel throat-socket.

All these mechanical factors are *passive potentials* for accomplishing the *"reduction of the vibratory mass"* but they do not automatically function on their own. *Only the singer can activate them* by correctly directing the *energized breath stream* into this lowest resonance cavity, and let the breath force grant these tones their "solidity factor". *But,* it is seldom understood that, the English language, as spoken by native Americans, creates a disadvantage for directing the breath stream, as is technically required, for American singers.

Generally, while speaking English, the breath stream automatically takes a *wrong* pathway, because the English language possesses a multiplicity of diphthongs *which are a singing disadvantage.* These diphthongs direct the breath stream incorrectly into the mouth cavity, then forward toward the front teeth, then out of the mouth.

Correct singing demands that the singer direct the breath stream far above the top note of the speaking voice's range of B♮ above middle C, for all females. Therefore, the singer must learn a very different method of directing the breath stream, which is—*backward and upward, into the posterior area of the mouth-pharynx cavity, then further upward, behind the soft and hard palates, and into the sinus and head cavities of the skull.* On the other hand, the Italian language, the ideal language for singing, operates almost exclusively on the so-called five "classic Italian vowels" *(oo) i (ee) e (eh) o (oh) and a (ah).* These "pure vowels" are the factors which enable *the breath stream,* for Italians, when speaking or singing, to rise *above* the top B♮ limits of the speaking voice's range, and to flow backward and upward into the mouth-pharynx cavity, and in some cases above it, into the head and sinus cavities of the skull.

This is what *William Shakespeare*, a well known singer and pupil of *Lamperti*, said about this matter, in his wonderful book—*The Art of Singing—1st edition 1899:*

"If English taught us sustained sounds and compelled a loose tongue, as Italian does, we should intuitively possess a higher standard of freedom of tongue and a sense of the open throat. But as the many vowels sounds of the English language are, on the contrary, far less sustained, and, together with our consonants, lead themselves to a throaty and blurred pronunciation, so that the difficulties of prolonging them with an open throat and loose tongue and lips, while speaking, becomes still more apparent when we try to sing!"

While singing, most of the physical maneuvers employed by the singer, in order to properly direct the breath stream, occur internally, and are therefore unseen by the singers' listeners. But, there occur other corresponding physical movements of the *cheeks, lips, and the muscles around the eyes*, which, as the singer accurately directs the breath into a selected resonance cavity, make highly visible movements. The external and visible cheeks, lips and the muscles around the eyes, correspond to and are the results of internal, muscular adjustments, which the singer instigates, and which are appropriate to the success of the singer's efforts to select the particular resonance cavity (s) to which the singer is directing the breath stream, in order to evoke a desired pitch.

Presently, in many American vocal studios, there has been a longtime, adamant protest directed at students, against their use of these involuntary facial movements, which are often but rather unconsciously called into play by vocal students. *But these teachers are dead wrong and don't know what they're talking about!* If any of them had ever been on stage, singing in a vocally challenging opera with another great singer, and taking note of certain facial muscles, which the singer was employing, they would have plainly seen for themselves that the great singer's facial movements were merely responding to other, unseen, internal muscular movements, which the singer was employing, in order to switch the breath stream from one resonance cavity to the next, and the throat-socket and vowel of one particular tone to the pitch and vowel-socket of another pitch.

Lilli Lehman called these switching of the breath maneuvers, *"break jerks!"*

William Shakespeare, the successful American singer, a star pupil of the great Italian teacher *Lamperti*, and the author of a wonderful and informative book, *The Art of Singing, Oliver Ditson Co., 1899, says the following:*

"The lips, while singing, are of great importance for indicating whether we are singing rightly or not. . .

"The command over the expression of the eyes depends upon the freedom of action of the muscles about the eyes, which raise the upper lip and act freely, if the face is free; but conversely, act rigidly, if the face is rigid. Therefore, the expression of the eye, while singing may be said to depend on the right or wrong method of producing the voice. The old Italian singing teachers used the phrase, "fior di labbra", or "flowering of the lips", when they wished to describe the unconscious smiling expression which is always associated with the very perfection of vocalization."

All the above physiological movements of the facial muscles, and the contributions of the various resonance cavities, necessary for the singer to achieve a precise calibration of a selected pitch, which result in the *"reduction of the vibratory mass", do not*, on their own, generate the calibration of accurate pitch, nor the reduction of the vibratory mass. The singer, alone, is the activator of these critical factors.

Hence, when the singer directs the breath stream into the tones of the *"Bottom Range"*, this lowest, shallow section of the complete *resonance channel,* and the least effective, of all the resonance chambers, its basic shape and size *merely <u>re</u>sounds, colors, and amplifies the original vibrations of the vocal cords,* but it doesn't originally produce them.

The "hookup points" that line the resonance channel

When we speak of the amount of *breath pressure* applied to any given tone, in order to evoke and develop that tone, doing so involves *stress!* Accurately and precisely applying stress must have a *focal* or *"hookup point"* toward which to direct the breath pressure, otherwise it becomes deflected and ineffective. These important *"hookup points"*, which line the length of resonance channel, must first be discovered by the singer, then developed to their maximum by using the swelled-tone exercise. The development of any selected tone, using the swelled-tone, and *its individual hookup point,* begins with the tiniest of *detached falsetto tones*, that produces a velvety, thin *fil di voce* or *"thread of voice"*, while also using the i (ee) and/or u (oo) vowels. These particular vowels, especially the detached falsetto i (ee), will reveal to the singer the precise, individual location of any particular hookup point, located along the full length of the resonance channel. The i (ee) vowel, reveals to the singer that, the *"hookup point"* of her selected tone occupies the smallest throat–space possible, and that the tones being evoked has no involvement with the lower register's muscles, nor any power.

For the singer to understand the precise location of a particular hookup point, the tone selected for exercise must be sung with the softest possible intensity, the purest vowel, and with a full, free, strong flow of breath continuously operating. When descending the range, using this extremely soft, *"ethereal"*, breathy, detached falsetto, open throated i (ee) vowel, each hookup spot of the singer's complete range may be precisely discovered, one by one. But once the sought after hook-up point has been discovered, there must be no haste on the singer's part to strength it, by applying the swelled-tone exercise, which would be prematurely.

The singer should instead occupy herself with allowing the breath force, for each newly discovered softly sung hook-up point, to flow freely through tone's throat-socket aperture, without the breath force being intensified, while allowing the tone to gradually invite incremental increases of the breath pressure, to strengthen the tone, at is own pace. Much later on, for a longer period of time than the singer would expect, when increased amounts of breath pressure applied to the selected tone's hook up point, to further strengthen it, the singer will readily understand if it is finally time to add the maximum breath pressure to a selected tone's hook-up point, because the selected tone the will no longer from its *precise focal point,* nor will its accompanying vowel distort from purity. If these positive responses do not occur, the singer must stop applying the maximum breath force to the tone, and return it to the softest possible volume. This will allow the singer to *relocate* the tone's precise *focal point,* and purify its vowel. Then much later, she can once again start the swelling process, to strength the tone's hook-up point, to its maximum potential.

The initial state of weakness of *a selected head voice, falsetto tone* conveys little of what can be eventually accomplished with it, through the swelled tone exercise. In the beginning, the sound of this tone will not be up to performance standards, nor should it be. However, with repeated applications of the swelled-tone exercise, over a long period of time, *(much long than most individual would imagine),* it will eventually become very strong, stable and controllable, and finally, when it had reached it advanced state of development, it connects itself to the power of the chest voice, and becomes very beautiful, all on its own. When any selected tone has been developed the tiniest, detached i (oo) vowel starting point, in the above prescribed manner, it automatically proportions the precise percentages of both registers, and it *"invites"* the lower register's *"solid core power"* to join the detached falsetto's starter-tone, in a team effort. This then represents the ideal version of the *messa di voce.* Each individual *hook-up point* has its own unique character, and it reacts differently to each of the five vowels, *u (oo), i (ee), e (eh), o (oh) and a (ah).*

In the post *Bel Canto* period, *a hookup point* a specific place along the resonance channel where the singer connects the *chest voice power* to the soft muscular controls of a detached falsetto, starter-head-tone was called *un gancio,* meaning in Italian, a *hook. When the detached starter-head tone reached an advanced state of development,* the old master teachers would instruct the singer to *"hook the chest voice power onto the small hookup point"* of the developed, falsetto, starter-tone. The student would also be told to, *"thread* the chest voice power through the starter-tone's "tiny" vowel-throat-socket, by swelling the tone's volume, accomplish with the help of the *mixed voice* mechanism and the breath force." After success has been had with any particular tone's hook-up point, the singer must rest her voice for a day or so, then, upon returning to her exercises, she should exclude the i (ee) vowel completely, and employ only the u (oo), o (oh) and/or AW vowels, all of which allow for the return of the full flow of the breath force, which the i (ee) vowel always tends to limit or completely stop.

The phenomenal "adjustability" of the resonance channel

It is interesting to note that, of all living creatures, *only human beings can adjust and connect larynx and pharynx together, in order to produce their speaking and singing voices.* This is possible because the muscles of the *pharyngeal-tract* posses an inherently malleable nature. The pharyngeal muscles may be exercised in various, that create various throat-socket shapes that can be adjusted to various positions, which the singer determines are necessary for singing purposes. These pharyngeal muscles, *(located distantly from the muscles that produce the various patterns of speech,* can be exercised in particular ways so that they produce throat shapes that are recognized as the *"instrumental vowels".* These instrumental vowels, when ideally produced, give the singer's listeners the illusion that they are hearing the same vowel patterns of normal speech.

There are vast differences between *what the singer muscularly must do, to produce pure superior tones,* then *add the precise elements of speech to them,* which we call *the singing vowels.* The reality of how this is accomplished is that, different sets of muscles accomplish each separate task. The muscles of the pharyngeal muscles, located in the upper, posterior area of the mouth-pharynx cavity produce the *pure vowels,* while the muscles of the lips, cheeks, and the tip of the tongue produce the consonants. Each separate group of muscles must first be located by the singer, then fully developed, but separately.

When changing a poor vocal condition to a superior one, the changes and adjustments which proper structuring accomplishes are made mainly to the *pharyngeal-tract* muscles, or the *head voice,* and *not to* the muscles of the chest voice. These pharyngeal muscles are located *within the resonating cavities of the mouth-pharynx and the sinus and head cavities* of the human anatomy. As their development advances, they can effect a permanent change with the muscular responses of *laryngeal notes, or the chest voice tones.*

Proper development of the *pharyngeal muscles* can be compared to the developmental methods employed by body-builders who hold that, the only way to develop muscles is through stressing them, by lifting weights, then allowing the exercised muscles to rest. With each successive exercise session, the muscles involved in a particular exercise must be more strenuously stressed than before, with heavier and heavier weights.

Singers, like weight-lifters, can apply progressively increasing stress to the vocal muscles that produce superior tone, and clear consonants, but it important that the singer understand that it is the *head voice muscles that should be stressed*, and <u>not</u> *the chest voice muscles.* And, instead of heavy, iron weights, of various pound ages, lifted by the weight lifter's arms, legs or other muscles, the singer, applies stress to a selected tone by attempting to pull the "power of the chest voice" from the bottom of the range, then upward along the resonance tract, until it reaches the position of selected starter-tone. Because the *detached falsetto muscles*, are to be stressed in the aforementioned manner, and they are initially weak and incapable of quickly accomplishing this task, the singer must gradually, over an extended period of time, lift the power of the chest voice, higher and higher, toward the falsetto, starter tone, with each separate exercises period, until the muscles of the head voice have achieved enough strength to lift the chest voice power *completely up* to the falsetto starter-tone, and connects it to the head- voice starter tone, thereby joined the muscular actions and tone qualities of both the chest and head voice together.

Understand, that this is accomplished by making the individual, detached falsetto tone's muscles the initiators of the "weight lifting process", while the chest voice's muscles are merely the passive participants, being lifted upward toward the starter-tone.

When the singer is performing the swelled-tone exercise, she is cautioned to apply only as much breath pressure as the underdeveloped, detached falsetto tone can tolerate, without it "cracking" away from the chest voice power, and shutting down. After she has succeeded in joining the chest power to the falsetto starter-tone, she must gradually diminish the stress which has applied to it, to accomplish that task, *by reducing the breath pressure from the starter tone,* which in turn brings the starter tone back its softest dynamic and stated of "detachment" from the power of the chest voice. The ultimate goal of the swelled-tone exercise is to gradually increase the swelling process so that greater "positive" amounts of the chest voice muscles' activities can be lifted up to original falsetto starter-tone. This is not possible until the starter tone's muscles have grown to their maximum strength. When this has been accomplished, the singer should be able to swell the detached falsetto tone to the maximum dynamic of *fff,* bringing the brilliant "core sound" of the chest voice's muscles into full and complete play, with the starter -tone.

This facility is not available until the original state of the chest voice muscles has been permanently transformed away from their original bulk and weight. However, only the full development of the pharyngeal tract can permanently transformed the chest voice, to a different form, one that "is thinner" and "lighter". Once transformed, the chest voice's tones appropriately adjusts themselves in *"weight" and "mass"* and *"throat-socket"* spaces. In this transformed state, they readily submit to being lifted upward in the range, then fitted into the smaller *(but now, not weak),* vowel-throat-spaces of the upper registers' throat-sockets. When the separate but now compatible *vowel-throat spaces of both registers* finally match each other, and smoothly *"fit together",* the altered muscles of both registers can *"hook up"* to each other, on each individual tone of the singer's complete vocal range. At that stage of development, all the muscles of two harmonic registers are capable of being *"clamped"* firmly together. With the two registers *"clamped together", (through the firm application of the breath force),* the singer can apply, at will, greater or lesser amounts of breath tension to her vocal cords, to satisfy the dynamic need (s) of the moment, for each individual tone of her range.

The terms *"vowel throat-sockets", "resonator shapes", "hookup-points", "clamps" "locks",* vowel throat- sockets, etc., come down to us from the historical past which produced the art of glorious singing. Here, they have been given updated names, and new twists of applications. All of them play critical roles in this manual's exercise program, for the cultivation of a superior singing instrument.

Most untrained singers refer to *the five classical vowels* as those which are produced when speaking. In some ways, spoken vowels are similar to the vocal sounds made when singing, but in many other ways *they are vastly different from those of the singing instrument. It is critical that these differences be clearly understood.*

In the beginning of training, the muscles which control the undeveloped *head tones* of the Top Range, *can not* operate throughout the singer's complete range, as they eventually should. *Their muscular controls must be calculatingly brought downward in the range* to "embrace" all the tones of the *bottom range.* After that has been accomplished, *they are still not strong enough* to grant the singer usage of the five instrumental vowels. Therefore, the five instrumental vowels must be individually developed by the *swell and diminish exercise.* This assignment takes a very long time to accomplish. As each individual tone gains strength, the singer is able to produce a closer version of an ideal, instrument vowel, than that particular pitch's tone's previous version of that same vowel. Meaning that, gaining an ideal version of each vowel is a process that begins with a predetermined idea of what that particular vowel will feel like, when developed to a state of ideal. However, its exact feeling, when it has been finally and ideally achieves, is rarely as the singer had envisioned it would be. The greatest obstacle for successfully accomplishing these *five pure vowels* is for the singer never to forget that the instrumental version of the five vowels differ greatly from the speaking voice's versions of each of them. And, that they will turn out to be vastly different, in form, and feel, than the singer had earlier imagined.

Considering that all the above, gaining success in creating the five instrumental vowels, turns out to be a longer, tedious, slow and ongoing process, than the beginner-singer expected it to be, at start training. Is it for these above reasons that most singers readily base their singing vowels on their speaking voice's vowels, since they already have a lot of experience in producing them, and it seems reasonable and easier for them to attempt to transfer the way she produces her speaking vowels, to the way she should produce her singing vowels. However, not only is this incorrect, but physically impossible! Total technical knowledge about the instrumental vowels, and how one technically comes to possess them, can only be had from the by slowly developing the head voice's muscles of control, while simultaneously urging their muscular throat-shapes toward the creation of each individual vowel, until each vowel reaches its highest standard of purity. Of course, if you're an American and your only language is English, this often requires the assistance of a native Italian voice teacher, whose primary language is Italian. Or a native Italian language teacher, whose primary language is also Italian.

Factors to be aware of when applying the messa di voce exercise

1. The vowel: Proper selection of an exercise's appropriate vowel, with regard to that vowel's potential, muscular effect upon the tone (s) being exercised.

2. The "attack": The correct way of initiating any selected tone.

3. Breath tension: The various ways of applying the motor force of *"breath tension", which* sets the vocal cords into motion, which then create the vocal cords' vibrations which are known as singing tones, or pitches, that also possess a dynamic range from soft to loud.

4. How to judge the muscular changes that take place, with the progressive development of the singing instrument:

    a) The physical sensations.

    b) The sounds that are internally heard, *only* by the singer herself.

    c) Properly interpreting, sensation-wise, what the singer feels and judges, about her vocal tones, as opposed to how her listeners hear and judge them.

The "vowel throat-sockets"

As the singer repeatedly applies the swelled-tone exercise to the vowel accompanies a selected tone, conveys a mental impression to the singer of the tone-and vowel's *size, shape, weight, and its precise focal* along the full length of the vocal tract, which is called the tone and vowel's throat socket. Because, in the beginning of training, each register's muscular system is antagonistic to the muscular system of the other register, the vowel throat-sockets of *each register* seem to the singer to have little, or no relationship to the other opposing register's vocal-throat-sockets.

    The vowel throat-sockets of the *chest register* are initially large and solid. And, they are very responsive to even a beginning singer efforts to explore them, but this can be misleading. And, another misleading impression is formed, because the chest register's throat-sockets easily gravitate to a specific and very tangible place in the singer's throat. *By contrast, the vowel throat sockets of the head register* are small, soft, and they are not nearly as responsive to the singer's efforts to explore them. Thee head register's tones seem to gravitate to *no specific place*, into which the singer can anchor any of them. Gradually coming to understand the *vast differences between the vowel throat-sockets of each individual register* serves the singer to a great advantage, especially when applying the "swelled-tone" exercise to any of them. Through many repeated applications of the *messa di voce,* with the detached falsetto pitches of the upper register, major changes will occur with the vowel throat-sockets of *both* registers, with regard to each individual throat-socket's progressively developing *strength, size, tonal textures, throat position,* and most importantly, *each vowel-throat-socket's relationship,* good or bad, to all the other tones of the singer's complete range.

An oscillating pattern of exercising both registers

During the long period of trying to bring the two antagonistic registers into harmony with each other, the synergistic nature of the registers sends *"muscular messages"* to the singer, through *vocal conflicts (often refereed to as muscular contractions),* which must be given full respect and be resolved. Singers with *partially structured* voices, whose singing is dominated by the muscular controls of but one register, are seldom aware of the synergistic needs of the two registers. This is so because the excluded register, for a long time, offers the singer no major conflicts, but eventually it will. When attempting to improve a voice of inferior structure, the functional contributions of both developing registers must be considered. Often, when the neglected register is finally considered, it immediately begins to sent signals to the singer, that it , too, now needs structural attention.

Thus far, we have been mainly concerned with exercising the falsetto voice. If the exercises given up to this section of the manual have been correctly applied, they will have advanced the inherently weak *head voice muscles* to a point where they are able to challenge the inherently dominant chest voice muscles. At that point, the synergistic needs of both registers demonstrate themselves most graphically. From then on, the singer must obey a new, *oscillating pattern of exercise*, giving her structural attention to each individual register, at separate exercises sessions.

As the singer continues to exercise the *head voice's falsetto muscles* with the swelled-tone exercises, a confrontation between the registers approaches. The advanced developed falsetto system may completely *"shut down"* the entire chest voice system. This occurs because, *the neglected chest voice register,* cannot be permanently denied, and it has finally *demand* the singer's complete attention.

Vocally instinctive singers sense this conflict and go about trying to resolved it as best as they can, calling upon whatever knowledge of the subject they possess. But, as the structuring of the two registers advances, the "war" between the two registers for dominance becomes even more critical. That's when the singer needs as much technical knowledge and assistance as she can find, to meet the crisis.

The need to adhere to the new, *oscillating pattern of exercising the voice* is generated by the registers themselves. Consequently, the singer is *obliged* to follow a "pendulum swing" pattern of exercising her voice—progressively *"updating"* each register's individual developmental needs, when *"that particular register demands her attention"*. She must guide each register away from its antagonism toward the opposite register, and towards a harmonious, cooperative state, through the use of particular exercises. If the singer has accomplished a high level of satisfactory development of the muscles of the head voice, this mandatory shift of attention *away from* the head voice muscles and *toward* the chest voice, has probably already begun to manifest itself, during the singer's daily exercise program. If so, it is likely that the application of the swelled-tone exercise, which had been granting the singer higher levels of success, has gradually become ineffective, without any apparent cause.

For any singer, presently in the above situation, the information above partially explains her, that which she has been confused about, struggling to understand— that she should temporarily put her work with the upper register aside, and now give her full structural attention to the neglected chest register.

One of the golden rules for dealing with the radical shifts that start to occur, with the advanced development of the two registers, is to use the airflow vowels u (oo), o (oh), and AW, exclusively for a while *(accompanying their applications by an increased amount of breath force)*, and to exclude the i (ee) and e (eh) vowels exercises, for a while. Doing so will establish some degree of harmony between warring registers, and grant back to the singer most of the tones of her complete range, which had become inaccessible. However, the confusing problem of these conflicting *"shifts"* and *"lock outs"*, from certain areas of the range, can only be permanently resolved by knowing how to resolve the problems of the *"vocal chasm"*.

The Vocal Chasm

When all singers sing upward from their Bottom Range toward their toward their Middle Range, they unavoidably encounter an *impasse*—the *"vocal chasm"*. *In actuality,* this *chasm* is located within *the lower, "true" passaggio..* For the singer, some tones situated *below this chasm*, are somewhat understandable; and so are all the tones, *situated far above The Middle range.* But the tones situated *within the chasm* are completely baffling. The specific tones of the *"vocal chasm" are illustrated below.*

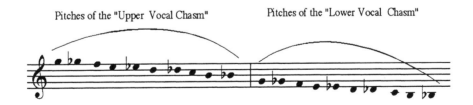

Pitches of the "Upper Vocal Chasm"   Pitches of the "Lower Vocal Chasm"

Remember that most female singers profess to have two *"passaggios"*—an *"upper passaggio"*, not the true passaggio, and a *"lower passaggio"*—which is the true passaggio. Considering this, then it stands to reason that most sopranos feel that they possess two "vocal chasms"—an *"Upper Chasm"*, and a *"Lower Chasm". See the illustrations above.*

Tongue and soft palate "arrangement" exercises for the tones of the "vocal chasm

From the first illustration below, select a detached falsetto tone, *(a tone that is totally devoid of resonant power),* located at the top of the vocal chasm, possibly the G♮2, or an even higher pitch, if it allows a greater amount of breath flow. Then *silently* adjust your throat's vowel-position to a fully open a (ah) vowel. This fully open a (ah) vowel's throat position remains unvoiced throughout the entire exercise. However, its throat position must be must silently establish and strictly maintained, in order to set up the proper throat-socket for the *second phase* of the exercise, which is to change the silent a (ah) vowel's throat-socket to a detached falsetto open i (ee) vowel's throat-socket, which will actually be sung.

Swelled tone exercises

"Vocal Chasm", single tone, descending exercises for all female voices

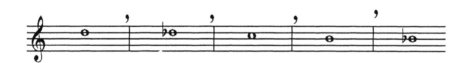

While changing from the *silent* open a (ah) vowel's throat position, to the open i (ee) vowel, look into a mirror and slightly raise your cheeks toward your eyes. Simultaneously, lift your tongue out of your lower throat channel and direct it into your mouth cavity. Once the tongue is there, allow your tongue's midsection to rise upward, toward the hard palate *(situated above it)*, and form a mound, then direct the tip of your tongue forward, toward the lower front teeth. *Most importantly, during the entire procedure of changing from the silent a (ah) vowel's throat position, to the i (ee) vowel, a great deal of breath must be continuously flowing.* These two Italian words,—*ciglio* and *signor*—when correctly pronounced, are very helpful for you to produce the *correct "pronunciation" of the detached falsetto,* open i (ee) vowel of this exercise. *Find a native Italian* and ask him/her to pronounce these two words for you, over and over.

Perform this exercise with all the tones of the *"upper vocal chasm"*, *one at a time,* as shown in the illustration above, *always in a descending direction!* Make no attempt to swell the tones, nor add *"core brilliance"* or *"power"* to them, for the time being. Then exercises these same tones with the pitches of the *lower "true" vocal chasm, at the bottom of the range.*

The next phase involves adding *"breath intensity"* to these same pitches. *Follow the instructions that follow. This 2nd phase of the exercise must not be tried until a great deal of time has been spend with the pitches of the 1ˢᵗ Phase.*

Adding *"breath-intensity"* to the vocal chasm's tones

After having successfully performed the *first phase* of this exercise, many times over, for *months or more,* in the manner described above, the singer is ready to add *"breath-intensity"* to them. *The goal of this first phase of the exercise* is to achieve a smooth, facile transition from the *silent,* open a (ah) vowel's throat-position, to the sung, open i (ee) vowel, while still trying to maintain the open a (ah) vowel's throat position. *The i (ee) vowel will cause the tongue to rise upward in the throat channel, which is appropriate,* then the singer must move its tip forward, toward the lower front teeth. A paramount factor with all these exercises is *to accompany all of them with a full, free strong flow of the breath, for each and every tone of the vocal chasm.*

To perform the *second phase* of these exercises, the singer must repeat all steps of the *first phase,* then with the *second phase,* slowly swells the volume of the open i (ee) vowel tone—but the singer must reserve enough breath force to diminish the *starter-tone* back to a soft intensity.

Do not rush these exercises, since they have an enormous effect on the entire vocal range. After applying these exercises, if the singer feels that her voice has suffered excessive stress, she should immediate rest her voice for a few days. Upon returning to her exploration of her voice, she should do some simple descending scales, employing the u (oo), o (oh), and A W vowels, and *exclude* the use of the i (ee) and e (eh), vowel. Then sing a few of the "Classic Songs", *(see pgs. 10 & 107).* It takes a very long time to completely structure the *lower "true" chasm* tones, *much longer than it does to structure the pitches of the "upper chasm".*

During the *first phase of the exercise,* a small muscle, situated in the *lower* throat, guided by the open throated, detached falsetto i (ee) vowel, will automatically and unavoidably connect itself to the larynx. As the singer increases the swelling process, this same muscle becomes taught and it communicates to the singer that the open i (ee) vowel has connected her larynx to her pharynx. As she increases the swelling process further, this thin, taut muscle moves the larynx *(and its power potential),* upward in the throat channel. Simultaneously, the starter-tone, far above, gradually repositions the soft palate downward and forward. Then, from far below, in the lower throat channel, the small falsetto i (ee) vowel's muscle, now been connected to the larynx, starts lifting the larynx upward a short distance, toward the top starter-tone. This upward movement of the *larynx may feel like a great distance to the singer,* but in fact the larynx has only been moved a very short distance. The singer then directs the movement of her larynx upward and *behind* her forward, and lowered soft palate. Positioning the larynx, up against the pharynx *creates a small, "gathered hinge point" which is the precise focal point* for the tone being presently sung. This *precise focal point* becomes the *transfer point,* for the presently exercised *tone.* This small, falsetto i (ee) *vowel*'s muscle, which has navigated the i (ee) vowel upward along the throat channel, has also established a *"thin line"* of connection between the larynx and pharynx, which the singer readily understands to be the precise pathway for all future ascending exercise scale or vocal phrase, when ascending from below the *lower passaggio,* into it, then ascending further upward, to the notes situated above it.

 This precise focal point is where the singer must focus the breath force, for the tone being presently sung, and similarly, thereafter, for all future tones of the *lower passaggio.* This specific spot is called the *"focal point",* or *point d'appui, by the French,* or the *punto d'appogiare, by the Italians.*

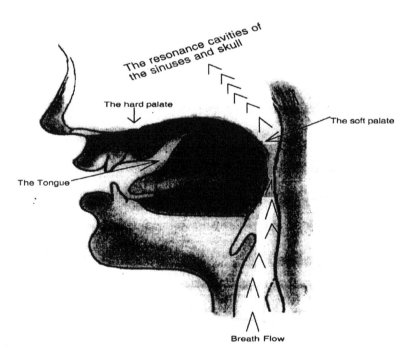

After the *"chasm"* has been completely restructured, *which takes quite a long time,* often years, it creates a *free passageway* for the *Breath Force,* rising out of the lungs, passing through the *glottis,* through the *Bottom Range,* then into the *passaggio itself, passing* behind the tongue and soft palate, then traveling further upward into the *nasal cavities of the sinus and skull.*

 If your throat and tongue respond unfavorably to these "Vocal Chasm" exercises, stop performing them and rest your voice for a good while. Upon returning to these exercises, eliminate the setting of the open throated a (ah) vowel's position, and the i (ee) vowel, completely, and use only the AW or the u (oo) vowels for all phases of the exercises.

Shifting the structural focus away from the head voice and toward the chest voice

Almost certainly the *"Vocal Chasm"* exercises, especially those that employ the *swelled tone* exercise, generate the need for the singer to start using an *"oscillating"* pattern of exercising her voice—by exercising the *Top Range for a while,* then shifting her attention away from the *Top Range and* over to the *Lower Range.*

The exercises that shift attention away from the muscles of the head voice and refocuses it upon the chest tones must be performed with u (oo), o (oh) and AW vowels, while *excluding* the i (ee) and e (eh) vowels, for a while. The u (oo), o (oh) and AW vowels enable the singer to restore the free the breath flow so that it may travel up and down the complete range, while the use of the open i (ee) vowel exercises, especially when a tone is swelled to develop its strength, tend to completely *"shut off"*. After the free flow of the breath stream has been reestablish, the singer may proceed to exercise the tones of her *Lower Vocal Chasm,* in a similar manner as was used to exercise the tones of the *Upper Vocal Chasm.*

In order to strengthen each individual note of the *vocal chasm* to an advanced level, the singer must *gradually and judiciously* increase the *breath intensity* of the selected tone. Eventually, the volume of the tone should be increased until the singer succeeds in *"pulling up"* all the core power and then connects it to the starter-tone. In that state, all three layers of depth of the vocal cords, are said to be operative at the same time. *(see pgs/ 123 & 124), "the three depths of vocal cord participation).*

But understand that, the exercise can only be considered successful when, after having connected the starter-tone to *full power,* the singer can completely *disconnect the core power from the starter-tone, and return the starter tone to a soft, puffy, detached falsetto tone.* While *"connecting"* and/or *"disconnecting"* the two registers to each other, *the singer must maintain a completely open throat, loose tongue, and a free flow of the breath stream.* During the process, all the lower range tones are rendered completely *"passive"* and *"hollow"* in order to allow the breath flow to *"whiz"* freely through them and arrive at the particular tone of the vocal chasm, being presently exercised.

After having exercised the tones of the *vocal chasm,* they have possibly restricted the breath flow through the *vocal chasm,* this is not unusual and it is only temporary. *Do not try to sing, immediately after a strenuous exercise period of this sort.* Let the throat muscles rest for a day or two, so they may readjust themselves to the new, beneficial effects of these exercises. Then perform some of the exercises below. Afterwards, sing some simple, classic songs, in order to observe the effects and results which the open i (ee) vowel exercises have had upon the entire vocal range. The exercises *below* are useful for reinstating the *"locked out"* pitches of the *Lower* and *Middle Ranges,* after performing many open i (ee) vowel *messa di voce exercises with the upper vocal chasm*, and they allow the breath to flow freely again. Their keys should be progressively lowered, to include more of the *Lower Range's tones.*

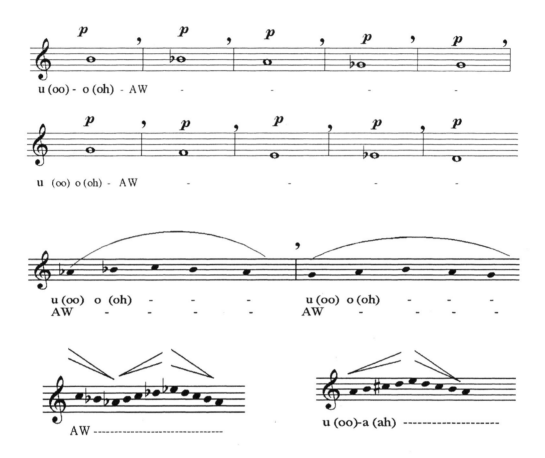

Eventually, you should lower and raise the keys of these exercises, in order to include more notes of the Bottom Range.

Relative to the exercises on the previous page, start with the u (oo) vowel, then gradually convert it to the o (oh) vowel's throat-space, then the AW vowel's throat space. Do not allow an *interruption of the breath* to occur when changing from the u (oo) to the o (oh) vowel. The *pp intensity must be maintained throughout the entire exercise.* The half tones, in-between these pitches *(not represented in the illustrations)*, must also be performed. The precise order in which these vowels are presented, with the u (oo) vowel first, followed by the o (oh) vowel, and ending with the AW vowel, *must be maintained.* Sometimes end the exercise with an a (ah) vowel, then stop to ponder its effects.

Manual Gracia, had this to say about *the soft palate.*

"Generally, all vocal timbres may be divided into two separate and distinct classes."

1) "The *bright*, clear and (*open throat*) timbres, and"

2) "The *dark*, (closed throat) timbres."

"These two, opposite qualities are principally obtained through the agency of the larynx and the soft palate. The movements of these two organs *are always in a contrary direction*. The larynx *rises* when the soft palate *falls*, and when the larynx *falls*, the soft palate *rises*."

"The *high vaulted soft palate* produces the *dark timbres*, and the lowered-and-forward position of the soft palate produces the <u>bright, clear timbres.</u> The high vaulted arch of the palate *rises* when we are *yawning*, and *falls* when we are in the act of *swallowing*."

"When the space between *the upper rear-mound of the tongue* and the soft palate separate themselves widely from each other, assuming the *"high vaulted"* position, they produce <u>*the dark, closed timbre.*</u>"

Manual Garcia Père also had this to say: "The real mouth of the singer ought to be considered the Pharynx."

Traitè Complet de l'Art du Chant, par Manuel Garcia, Père, *Paris, 1840*

Enrico Caruso said: "Practicing certain tones with a closed mouth, when it can be done safely, is all that is really necessary to correctly place certain tones."

Beniamino Gigli, the great Italian tenor, had this to say:
"The EE vowels on the lower and medium notes are narrow, and are posteriorly, produced sounds, (at the back of the throat, author's comment), and not forward, as when speaking. But once we are on the high pitches they must be ample space created for (their) development, just as if they were the same "aperture" as the AH vowel, which is space-providing, for purposes of tonal amplification, and made primarily with the mind and the will of the singer (cervella e volontà)."

After the singer has connected the open-throated i (ee) vowel to the open a (ah) vowel, she will feel that a small, unobtrusive connection has been made between the larynx, below, and pharynx, above. The singer must *"clamp"* the i (ee) vowel to the a (ah) vowel's throat positions firmly together with the force of the breath pressure. Successfully doing so will assure the singer that she has properly joined the *chest register (pharyngeal connection),* and *head register (laryngeal connection),* together.

During past, great vocal training periods, this *"clamping together process"* of the *chest voice* and *head voice* muscles together was referred to as *fiato ferma,* or *"holding* the *chest* and *head voice* muscles tightly together with *firm breath support"*. Clamping the *pharynx* and *larynx* together, and the *reverse maneuver* of "unclamping them", are the only means which the singer has of synergistically employing and controlling the muscular contributions of *both the chest and head voice registers.*

Knowing how to properly direct *the energized air stream* into various resonance cavities, located along the length of the *resonance channel, (which entails visible movements of the cheeks and lips, and the unseen soft palate),* grants the singer the ability to circumvent the antagonism which the *chest voice* and *head voice* perpetually hold toward each other. These movements of the cheeks, lips, and soft palate also participate in accomplishing the thickness/thinness, shortening/lengthening process of the vocal cords, critical for individually calibrated each pitch of the singer's complete vocal range. Factors which the speaking voice *can never accomplish*, and which presently, are not even remotely considered!

Relative to the *messa di voce exercise, Manuel Garcia Père* advised:

"The *messa di voce must not* be performed at the beginning of training. It is most difficult to swell a note, passing smoothly from the *head voice* to the *chest voice.* At first it may be necessary to cut this exercise in half, to swell a tone in one breath, and diminish it with *a new breath.* But once it has been mastered, it is of great use with the upper *passaggio* tones of *E♭, E♮, F♮, F♯ and G♮.*"

Garcia did not specify why he advised the above. But for sure, he clearly understood that if the *messa di voce* exercise is applied prematurely, *before* a selected tone has been fully saturation with the Breath Flow, it will bring too much chest power into play. Consequently, the muscles of the *head voice, which are responsible for loosely holding the vowel socket of the throat fully (as well as grating a loose tongue),* would collapse.

If you want to learn more about the *messa di voce* exercise, read my 1995 vocal manual, *A Singer's Notebook,* which may be purchased at Patelsen's Music Store, 160 West 56th street, Manhattan, NY, Zip-10019, Tel: (212) 757-5587.

The inherently "thinner" contours of the Tops Range's tones

Here are some mental images that may guide the singer toward the proper execution of all ascending scales:

1) The singer should start the scale with the smallest possible, yet energized focal point *(throat space)* in mind; of the five vowels, the open, detached falsetto i (ee) vowel is the most helpful to accomplish that end. Some singers fare better by using the u (oo) vowel.

2) The singer must think that she is threading the i (ee) vowel (energized exclusively by the breath flow), into the throat-socket of a "puffy" u (oo) vowel.

3) As the singer initiates the ascending movement, she energizes the tone, continuously channeling it into the narrower passageway of the head voice tract. This thinner tract's muscular contours will seem initially *hollow and weak*, by comparison with the contour of the chest voice, but in time they will grow to be very strong, precisely felt, and clearly understood by the singer, through mental imagery.

This thinner tract guides the singer to performing a correct ascending scale. This *"thinness factor"* physically denies the thicker throat-sockets of the *chest voice*, and "compresses" them into narrower version of themselves, without compromising quality of the tone (s), nor purity of the vowels.

When performing ascending scales, the singer must continuously readjust "power and throat-shape" to this "thinning" process. This is *not* merely a mental adjustment, but *an actual* physiological one. The failure of the singer to acknowledge and yield to the *"thinning process"* as she ascends her range, will encounter "road blocks', and in of the advanced develop head some cases, totally denying of the ascent.

Figure 3

$$p \underset{}{\overbrace{}} f \underset{}{\overbrace{}} p \underset{}{\overbrace{}} ff$$

The *esclamazio languida*

All ascending vocal movement automatically creates a merger of the muscular actions of both registers. When acting together in unison, the registers form a highly desirable *"collaboration"* on every individual tone of the complete range. A *velvety quality* is contributed by the head voice, and a *sparkling, core brilliance* is contributed by the chest voice. The old master teachers called this merger *chiaroscuro (clear and bright), a tone with a bright center and a dark rim*, or *a tone with a dark center and a bright rim.* When the initially antagonistic registers finally function together with total muscular harmony, as is necessary for the success of all ascending vocal movement, they grant the singer complete control of all dynamics. This muscular harmony also grants the ascending scale or vocal phrase smoothness of vocal movement, in both ascending and descending directions.

The illustration below shows how, when performing an ascending scale, the lower register's throat space must be consciously "gathered" by the singer and be "threaded" into the *narrower channel* of the vocal tract passageway. Then the lowers registers is physically forced to relinquish its thickness and readily adapt itself to the thinner muscular contours of the vocal tract's passageway.

The contours of the head voice's passageway are actually the advanced structured pharyngeal muscles *(all the advanced developed falsetto tones)*, which have been

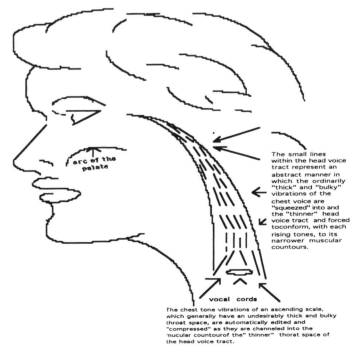

arc of the palate

The small lines within the head voice tract represent an abstract manner in which the ordinarily "thick" and "bulky" vibrations of the chest voice are "squeezed" into and the "thinner" head voice tract and forced toconform, with each rising tones, to its narrower muscular countours.

vocal cords

The chest tone vibrations of an ascending scale, which generally have an undesirably thick and bulky throat space, are automatically edited and "compressed" as they are channeled into the mucular countourof the" thinner" thorat space of the head voice tract.

developed by the swelled-tone exercises, and then that muscular development must be transported downward in the range and made to overlap all the tones of the *chest voice*, to create a strong muscular *"head voice ramp."*

The manner in which all ascending scales travel upward and downward along this *"head voice ramp"* should be considered. Understand that the unwieldy, "solid action" of the chest voice, which accompanies all ascending vocal movement, *must be first gathered, then made to curve vertically backward and upward,* following a pathway similar to the inner curve of the C *alphabet,* or the shape of *a crescent, new moon.* The energized *breath stream,* which *"motors"* the scale upward along the resonance channel, must consciously be made to pass behind the soft palate, then behind the arc of the hard palate, then directed toward the resonator cavities of the mouth-pharynx and/or head and sinuses, which ever one is appropriate for the presently sung tone.

All ascending scales automatically utilize the dynamics of breath tension defined by the *esclamazio languida* exercise. Unlike the *descending scales,* of the developing detached falsetto exercises, which require *a lesser amount* of breath pressure, *all ascending scales* demand incremental increases of breath pressure to satisfy the rise in pitch. Also, the bulk of the chest voice must be reduced with each successive pitch through a series quickly executed, alternating muscular *"compressions"*, *"lifts"* and *"rests"* and "repositionings" of *throat-socket maneuvers*, relative to the pitch and the amount of breath pressure necessary to produce it. This asks for much skill in applying and reducing the breath pressure, then applying it again, in quick, alternating applications.

The best place in the range to start the first *ascending scales* is as close as possible to C2. The present structural goal is to attach the action of the chest voice *(which has been purposefully withheld until now),* to the tones of each scale. However, it is *still* desirable to engage a lesser amount of chest voice activity at this phase. This critical, precautious approach helps the singer to avoid bringing into play the maximum action of the chest voice. This insures that any beneficial muscular influences already gained with the swelled-tone exercises *will not* be excessively burdened by an *"overload"* of chest voice's weight.

If the necessary dominance of the advanced falsetto's muscular controls, over the chest voice muscles' controls *has not* been established with the C2 pitch, the singer will likely meet with resistance, when attempting to couple the *"solid"* muscular controls of the chest voice to the soft, puffy, falsetto "starter-tone" and the connection will possibly be denied. All this may seem odd, but it is often indigenous to the first attempts with the *"connecting process"*, and must *not* be considered a negative factor. The resistance of both registers to be connected to each other mirrors the response which the chest voice muscles originally displayed, when the singer originally began to apply the muscular controls of the head voice to them. The proper *"attack"* or *"starting process"* of connecting the two registers together, after they have arrived at their most advanced stage of development, has always been a "tricky" factor. Even, as far back in time to the Post *Bel Canto* period.

For a soprano to accomplish a proper *"attack"* she was advised to employ a soft breath pressure to the tone, in the manner of a sigh, which was then quickly followed by a strong pressure, in the manner of a gentle hammer blow, a *"martello"* (Italian for, *"a small hammer"*) , in order to bring the two resistant registers to a state of connection with each other. However, if the first *"starter-tone"* of a selected ascending scale *does not resist* the "coupling" process, the singer will easily succeed with the connecting process and she is ready to perform any of the forthcoming ascending scales. If there is resistance, then she should use the *"martello"*, or small hammer.

Guidelines for your "attacks"

1) If your initial attempt to attach chest power to the first tone of an ascending scale meets with failure, you may get a *false impression* that it would be better *not* to add the chest power to that tone, at all. This experience is rather commonplace, for many female singers. However, attaching the chest voice to the softer falsetto starter-tone *must be accomplished*, if the ascending scale is to be performed correctly and safely, and synergistically.

2) When trying to couple the power of the chest voice to the falsetto starter-tone of an ascending scale, resistance to doing so may occur when the singer has spent a long time, during many exercise sessions, developing her falsetto register's muscles, while having purposefully neglected the tones of the chest voice, as she has been advised to do, by this manual.

In order to be successful with your "attack", you may be obliged to *temporarily bypass the preferred soft approach to connecting the chest power to the starter-tone*, and instead *firmly "lean"* or *"press"* the vibrant quality of the chest voice into the resistant falsetto starter-tone, while not forgetting to keep the breath flowing throughout the process. In some instances, this firm *"leaning"* or *"pressing"* action must be aggressively applied, more firmly so, than seems rational. In this way, using the approach of the *"martello"* or small hammer, the resistant, *falsetto* starter-tone can be insistently made to couple with the *action of the chest voice.*

When all the tones of the ascending scale are ready to utilize the muscular controls of *both registers*, it signifies that the singer has successfully departed from using the singing instrument in the *detached mode,* which is generally used for many of exercises, at the beginning phase of structuring her voice, and has now successfully placed the singing voice in the *connected mode*, used for performing.

This forceful *leaning* into the falsetto starter-tone of an ascending scale, with a firm breath tension *"attack"* was termed, by the old master teachers of the past, *appoggiare la voce.* In English this means "to lean *(the pressure of the breath),* upon the voice" *(the vocal cords).* The later teachers of the *Neapolitan and Paris periods* of vocal training were also aware of both the *"detached mode"* and the *"connected mode"* of the singing instrument. They were also familiar with the insistent method that a singer sometimes had to use, a stroke of the *"martello"*, in order to bring her voice from the detached mode into the *connected mode*. During the Paris years of *Jean de Reszke and Giovanni Sbriglia,* this approach to connecting the two registers was called, the *"coup de glotte"*, a stroke of the glottis.

Ascending vocal movement &
The upward pulls of the advanced developed falsetto tones

The *upward pulling action* of the *advanced-developed falsetto voice* can be compared to the wound-up spring of a clock. *This upward-pulling action may first reveal itself to the singer when she is trying to "bind" the falsetto, head voice starter-tone to the power of the chest voice. When that is the situation, and as the singer starts the process of clamping the power factor to her advanced developed, starter-falsetto tone, to her surprise, the starter tone pulls upward and away from her attempt to clamp it to the power factor, and whizzes upward toward the top of her range.*

This upward, falsetto pull is very valuable. Once the singer has succeeded in clamping the starter-tone to the upward-pulling factor, and begins the ascending vocal phrase, the upward pulling muscles of the head voice starts to accomplish at least *95%* of the "work load" of the scale's ascent for her, and with minimal effort. This upward-pulling factor grants the ascending scale superior tone, precise intonation and total ease of ascent, as opposed to the *strained, "pushed up" unmusical* effect frequently manifested, when an ascending scale is "forced" upward in the range by *forced resonance, which occurs when the head voice's upward pulling action is not available to the singer.*

These *"upward pulls"* transport *only* the *"transportable"* or *"adjustable"* power of the chest voice, but not its the raw, weighty, and negative factors. *The "transportable factor of the chest voice"* is actually the highly kinetic vibrations of the vocal cords' mixing themselves with the strong kinetic currents of the breath force, then together, traveling rapidly upward along the resonance channel.

The upward *forcing* of ascending scales and vocal phrases by most present-day vocal students *can be eliminated.* But, that can only happen when power of the chest voice have been made *"movable" and "adjustable" and "kinetic"* The particular vowel which most reveals the nature of the upward pulling muscles of the head voice is the open, falsetto i (ee) vowel. When this particular i (ee) vowel is properly created, at the top of the soprano's range, F2 upward in the range to B2, and fully developed, it creates this upward pulling action, from the very beginning of it first being strengthened, and immediately starts grants the singer the use of these valuable, *upward pulling muscles.* If the singer does not get quick sense of this particular i (ee) vowel's *upward pulling potential,* then she has not yet evoked a proper, pure, detached falsetto (i) vowel which comes to exist and thrives on strong breath currents, and can *only* be evoked with a combination of *"brain and will power",* as the great Italian tenor, *Beniamino Gigli,* was fond of saying.

Here is *a scenario* which explains how this works. With an *incorrect attempt* at performing an *ascending scale,* the singer goes directly to the bottom of her range to start the ascending scale, but she does not access the upward pulling, open i (ee) vowel help at all, since she hasn't the least idea that such a factor is available to her. Therefore, starts the ascending scale with a raw, tone, which totally devoid of any head voice "blending" Because of that missing element, she is only able to produce an inferior, unmusical, "unwieldy", "forced resonance" ascending scale.

Conversely, here is a scenario which follows the *correct manner* of singing an ascending scale. The singer goes to the bottom of her range, to evoke the *"starter-tone"* of her ascending scale, but she is very cautious in doing so, and mindful that she is searching for a particular kind of starter tone, one that is "mixed", with the muscular action soft the head voice and possesses the "upward pulling" actions of the developed head voice, which, as soon as she applies the breath pressure to the starter-tone of the scale, will energetically start rising upward, towards the very top of her range.

But this correct starter-tone will always react to the breath force, in two possible ways. In one way, when the singer *is unsuccessful* in her attempt to attach the movable chest voice's power to the starter-tone, however, and the head voice will not submit to being connected, and instead "zip" upward to the Top Range, *without* its "passenger"—the movable chest voice. Conversely, with the second way, when the singer has *successfully connected the power of the chest voice to the correct starter tone*, it allow the singer to connect the power to it then immediately starts its ascending motion, with approximately 90% the *"work load"* being handled by the head voice's upward pulling actions.

The singer should now put the above knowledge to a test.

The singer evokes the starter-tone of a simple five-tone, ascending scale, and establishes an AW vowel with it. Then she *"threads"* a detached falsetto i (ee) vowel through the AW vowel's throat socket, and with it, she starts the ascending scale. The ascending scale immediately glides upward in the range, being pulled along by the muscles of the *developed falsetto voice*, which has been accomplished though many applications of the detached falsetto i (ee) vowel. As the scale moves along, what is revealed to the singer is that, each higher pitch of the ascending scale is being helped to accomplish a smooth and almost effortless ascent along a *"thin, curved, ascending pathway"*, towards the top pitch of the scale, as if all the pitches of the scale were traveling on a gliding escalator, and were totally free from any downward, antagonistic pull of the chest voice. The singer should rest her voice for a few minutes then perform this same simple, five-tone ascending scale, but this second time, using the u (oo) vowel, which will help the singer to more clearly and fully understand the upward-pulling action of the advanced falsetto head voice's help, since with the u (oo) vowel, the *"work load"* of the ascending scale has been reduced to its minimum.

While performing any and all ascending scales, the chest voice muscles are *not free from any duty,* since they must perform two factors that are critical to the success of the ascending scale:

1) The chest voice muscles must add brilliance to all the tones of the ascending scale, and—

2) The chest voice muscles must contribute a downward, *counter-pull* to the head voice's continuous *upward pulling action,* in order for the singer to perform a descending scale.

In these two ways, each individual register may continuously interact with the other register, in order to accomplish both the *upward pulling* and *downward pulling* movements of each individual register. If it were not for the existence of these *upward and downward pulling controls* of the two registers, there would be no way for the singer to achieve precise ascending or descending vocal movements.

The gathered voice

Generally, if a singer sings *"flat"*, she generally does not have enough *upward-pulling* head voice control available to her, in order to lift the *"flat"* tone to its precise vibrations level, and to accomplish its precise pitch. In that situation, the tone is said to be *"flat"*, and under pitch. Conversely, when the singers sings "sharp", there is generally not enough *downward pull*, by the chest voice, to lower the tone to its precise intonation level of vibrations.

In the beginning, the head voice's *upward pulling* action often makes the execution of an ascending scale *bumpy* and *irregular.* This will happen when the singer doesn't have sufficient experience and skill in controlling the air flow that generates the pitches of the rising scale or vocal phrase. As the tones of the ascending scale rise upward in the range, they demand an increase of breath tension, which adds yet another complex factor to the ascending scale. This mandatory increase of breath tension is particularly troublesome as the ascending scale encounters the borders of the various, different vocal zones, and especially so, in the area of the registers' break. When these borders are met and *not* properly crossed, unpleasant sounds and audible gaps occur, with the singing.

The "gathered voice"

All ascending scales must function in a easy-flowing, smooth manner. But, only those singers with advanced *head voice* development, who possess masterful skill in managing the breath flow, and who possess the head voice's upward pulling actions, can sing a precise, *"seamless"* ascending or descending scale.

Experienced singers, with well-developed voices, give their listeners a false impression that their seamless vocal scale is *"effortless"* to produce. This is an illusion created by the skillful singer. Whereas, the singer is actually dealing with a challenging physiological reality that is anything but effortless. The greatest challenge to smooth, superior singing is created at the most advanced stage of development, when the power of the chest voice is fully connect to the advanced-developed, falsetto tones. At first, it is difficult for the signer to adjust the to the new, muscular contributions of chest register; since, while actually singing, at one moment, there seems to be too *much "chest voice";* and at other moment *"too much head voice."* The singer's skill stabilizing her voice, by applying *only* the precise amount of either the *chest voice* or *head voice's* muscular contributions, must become consistent. This is the dream of all singers, but the actual attainment of but a few. Adding the full participation of the chest voice power to each and every tone of the singer's complete range will bring temporary, disruptive energy into play, but this must be accomplished, and its consequential cumbersome influence must be properly managed and concealed from the singer's listeners.

This disruptiveness becomes more intense when the singer passes from a lower pitch to a higher one. This is so because the singer must increase the amount of breath-pressure being applied to the vocal cords. This unavoidably adds more energy to the vocal production, and a higher probability for greater vocal disruptiveness. In the beginning, the incremental increases of breath-pressure tends to create unmusical, discordant vocal sounds. However, with skill and the passing of time, these disruptive, raw, unpleasant sounds can be transformed into highly musical, harmonious, superior vocal sounds. Accomplishing superior, harmonious vocal sounds is usually the "job" *of the hollow u (oo) vowel, and the open o (oh) vowel (the two "rounding-off" tools of voice training),* and superior skill at handling the various dynamics of the breath flow.

The "rounding off" of the singing voice, after it has reached an advanced state, can be accomplished, in part, by performing exercises individually sustained pitches that begin with a soft, closed u (oo) vowel, then gradually changing its throat-socket to an open a (oh) vowel, then changing it to an AW vowel, then swelling and diminishing the swelling the AW vowel to an *fff* dynamic, then gradually diminishing it back to a *ppp dynamic.* Sometimes the singer should pass from the o (oh) vowel to an a (ah) vowel, instead of the AW vowel, then swell and diminished the a (ah) vowel, in the same manner prescribed above for the AW vowel.

More about ascending vocal movement

All ascending vocal movement can be potentially injurious to the singing instrument if all the various sections of the complete range don't function muscularly harmoniously with each other. To judge whether the total range of the singer's voice has been properly aligned, it is necessary to perform a series of ascending scales. Many singers assume that the ascending scale exercise is a *voice builder*, but they are wrong. The ascending scale is rather *a test*, to see if each and every tone of the complete range is muscularly harmonious with all its neighboring tones. During past great periods of vocal training, when making a test of the total range's proper aligned, the singer was told, by the old, grand master teachers to perform *"The Grand Scale"*, in order for the singer to observe several critical factors:

1) To note if the "upward pulls", created by the advanced developed, "detached falsetto" open i (ee) vowel are operative with each and every successive, ascending tone of an ascending scale, and if each vowel is being placed accurately into its precise vowel throat-socket, which renders the purest form of both vowel and throat-socket.

2) To question whether or not the inherent "bulk" or "mass" of the chest voice is being continuously reduced—known as *"the reduction of the vibrator mass factor"*—as the scale rises upward in the range. This desirable *reduction of the vibratory mass*, can only be accomplished if the singer makes a conscious effort to *"thread"* each successive, higher tone into the thinner muscular contours of the head voice tract.

3) To note, when an ascending scale approaches the *passaggio*, with its critical *"cross over tones"*— E♭, E♮, F♮ F♯, if the singer manages to properly transfer the *"work load"* of each successive ascending tone, away from the chest voice's muscular controls, and over to the muscular controls of the *head voice*. A quick "puff of breath", emitted just before evoking each successive higher tone, will help to accomplish this.

For the muscles of the head voice to achieve these superior controls of the passaggio tones, they require many years of development, during which time, the singer must patiently endeavor to increase the muscular strength of the falsetto muscles in the upper half of the vocal range. During this long period, the singer must switch her attention back and forth between *developing the detached falsetto's muscular system, at the top of her range*, and adjusting *chest voice's muscular system, at the bottom of the range, to update the influences which the advancing head voice development has had upon it.*

When the *"work load"* demanded by ascending scales has been reduced to its minimum, it is because the singer has developed her *"mixed voice"* to its maximum strength. This grants all her tones *"buoyancy"*, *"flexibility of movement"*, and their ideal *tonal color*. The master-teachers of the past said this about the "ideal tonal quality" of each tone of complete vocal range, that they should possess "*chiaroscuro.*" Literally translated, *chiaroscuro* means *clear and dark—the inherent "darkness" of the head voice, and the clear "brightness" of the chest voice.*

Simple ascending scale exercises

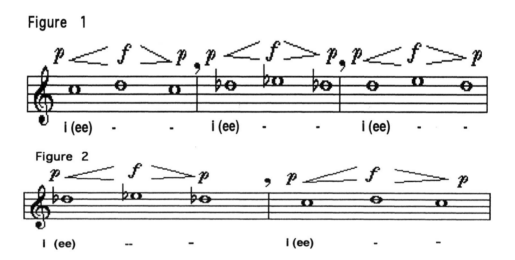

With *figures 1 and 2* we present the *first ascending scales* which transfer the singing voice from the *detached mode* to the *connected mode.* This grants to the singer the *"performing voice"*. Use an open i (ee) vowel, which has been threaded through a fully open-throated a (ah) vowel, and infuse the tone with a strong breath flow. Direct the tone backward, toward the posterior area of the mouth-pharynx, then further upward, behind the soft and hard palates. The singer is encouraged to experiment with the all the remaining vowels, settling with the particular one that enables her to obtain the best results.

With *Figure 3 (below),* there occurs an unavoidably, critical *Vocal Zone* change between the first and second notes of the first and third measures. While ascending the pattern, the singer must assure that a smooth transition *is accomplished between the first and second notes.* If this is not possible, it indicates that these first two tones do not possess enough "head voice dominance" to guide the chest voice's power harmoniously up the top note. Therefore, these tones should be further strengthened individually and separately through use of the swelled-tone exercise with the hollow u (oo) vowel.

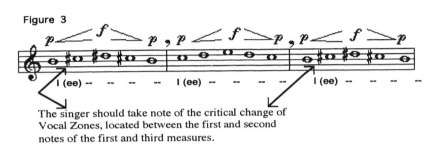

Figure 3

The singer should take note of the critical change of
Vocal Zones, located between the first and second
notes of the first and third measures.

Figure 4

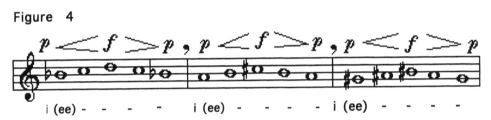

i (ee) - - - - i (ee) - - - - i (ee) - - - -

Observe that in *Figure 4 (above),* each successively lower, starting-tone, of each new measure, automatically adds an increased amount of chest power to the scale. Though the intention of these ascending scales is to add the "bite" or "solidity" of the chest voice to the scale, that bite and solidity must not deny the singer a smooth transition from one note to the next. If a vocal *"blockage"* or *"denial"* of a smooth passage upward occurs, *do not* complete the scale. Instead, return to performing some *"detached falsetto"* descending scale exercises, for a while which involved the underdeveloped tones. By reversing the upward direction of each pattern, to the downward direction, that will automatically brings the falsetto's beneficial influence downward in the rang, which it desirous. The *u (oo)* and *i (ee)* vowels are best for these restorative, descending *detached falsetto* scales.

Figure 5

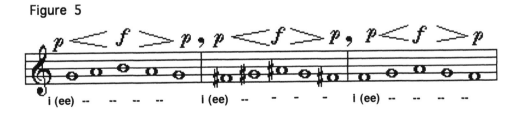

i (ee) -- -- -- -- i (ee) -- - - - i (ee) -- -- -- --

Figure 6

i (ee) -- -- -- -- -- -- --- --   i (ee) -- -- -- -- -- -- --

Figure 7

i (ee) - - - - - - -   i (ee) - - - - - - -

When performing the scales of *Figure 5* assure that the F♯ sharp and F♮ starting tones *of the 2nd and 3rd measures* are muscularly pure, meaning, free from any conflicts with the tones above and/or below them. Frequently, with these two particular low tones the singer incorrectly calls into play some excessive chest register action, which denies these tones their need to be totally, *head voice dominated.*

Figure 8

i (ee) - - - - - - -

The singer should experiment with the exercises of *Figures 1, 2, 3, 4, and 5,* by lowering and raising their keys, so that they encompass more pitches of the range. With some of these scales, the singer may discover *"dull, hollow spots"* which *lack the required resonant vibrato action.* That is temporarily acceptable. To correctly add the *missing* resonant vibrato action to these *"dulled tones"* perform the ideal passage through the vowels' exercise *(pg. 29).* Afterwards, the ascending scale should be performed again, to observe whether the *"gaps"* and *"hollow spots"* have been removed. Remember, when performing any ascending scale, it is important to ensure that the *mixed voice (an advanced developed falsetto tone that "sounds and feels like" a chest tone, but is actually a falsetto tone),* is employed to transfer the power of the chest voice from each lower pitch to the next higher pitch, of the ascending scale. Before performing the next sets of ascending scales, it would be beneficial for the singer to perform a series of descending five-tone scales. This should be done with the detached falsetto voice, using both the u (oo) and i (ee) vowels, starting at the upper part of the range.

The next set of ascending scales have a highly beneficial twist to them. Rather than starting the scale at the bottom tone then ascending to the top tone, *they start at the top of the pattern,* utilizing the top pitch as a "tuner" for the forthcoming descent. Upon reaching the lowest tones of the descent, ascend back upward to the top of the pattern, following the same path that was experienced when descending the scale. By starting these scales with the top tone, it assures that the scale is started with maximum head voice, muscular purity *(meaning, no negative downward pulls are bulk and weight from the chest voice's muscular controls)*.

The exercises of *Figures 6, 7, & 8 (above)* should be started with a *mezzo-forte* dynamic. As the singer descends the scale, the volume must be gradually reduced to a *pianissimo*. Upon arriving at the lowest tone, the singer must *not* to take a new breath, but instead, immediately ascend the scale, while gradually increasing its volume, until a *fortissimo* is accomplished with the top note.

The exercises of *Figures 9, 10, and 11 (below)* prepare the singer for actual singing. With them, he can *"set up"* the most advantageous condition of the complete vocal range, for purposes of performance. These scales grant the singer a consistently reliable method of evaluating the vocal instrument's readiness to start singing. These exercises consist of first selecting critically located tones, and sustaining them, judge their accuracy. The singer then performs the ideal *passage of the five vowels*, with any tones that passes his judgment, which starts with the *u (oo) vowel, followed by the i (ee), e (eh), (oh), and a (ah) vowels*, smoothly changing from one vowel to the next *without taking a new breath*.

Figure 9

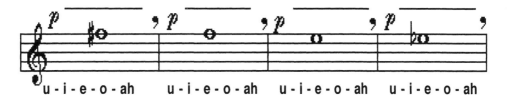

u - i - e - o - ah   u - i - e - o - ah   u - i - e - o - ah   u - i - e - o - ah

Figure 10

u - i - e - o - a   u - i - e - o - a   u - i - e - o - a   u - i - e - o - a

Figure 11

u - i - e - o - a   u - i - e - o - a   u - i - e - o - a   u - i - e - o - a

It is permissible and often practical, and sometimes essential for singers to exercise their singing voices with *one particular vowel* for a prolonged period of time, while neglecting the other four vowels, in order to accomplish a specific purpose. However, doing so is a temporary *departure* from *"nature's way"* of maintaining *vocal health* and the efficient function of the singing voice. *"Nature's way"* is *to keep all five vowels continuously operative*, and acting as a team to maintain correct *"checks and balances"* between the vowels, and of *the other singing organs.* After a prolonged period of vocal exercising *with one particular vowel*, and prior to singing repertoire, the singer must perform the *ideal passage of the five vowels* on sustained tones, until all tones considered critical for performing have once again adjusted to the participation of all five vowel.

With the *ideal passage of the five vowels,* the registers' precise percentages *(how much chest voice and/or head voice should be used)* will be automatically set into precise order.

Getting ready to sing, after vocalization

The above ascending scales are some of the oldest and most beneficial exercises ever created by the old master teachers. After first developing the muscles of the upper register muscles *to their maximum potential*, they must be united with those of the lower register. The performance of these *ascending scales* is invaluable for bringing the two registers into a *"connected"* state of harmonious interaction with each other. This "connected *mode" brings* all the muscular functions of the entire singing instrument into play, so that they function as a single, *harmonic* unit. *This is critical to the "performing mode" of the vocal instrument.* For the beginning singer, the "warm up" process may take an hour or so to properly accomplish, other times less. As the singing voice's develops, the amount of time necessary for the "warm up" period will greatly diminish.

The classic songs and arias of the Seventeenth and Eighteenth Centuries

Some of the most vocally beneficial performance pieces are the *Twenty-four Italian Songs and Arias of the Seventeenth and Eighteenth Century.* They can be readily found in a single collection at any reputable music store. Here is a list of those I recommend. I have divided them into *two categories*; those songs with *slow sustained movement*, and those with *fast vocal movement.* Singers, whose voices are trained in a manner that *includes* the muscular actions and qualities of *both registers* often find these songs highly beneficial to the development and discovery of their singing voices, and a delight to perform. Singers who rely exclusively on the chest voice "ascending scales method" of voice training, which produces *"thick tones"* and *"limited control of dynamics"*, generally find them *"difficult"*, *"boring"*, and *"useless"*.

Of course, their negative attitude toward these masterpieces is understandable, since an incorrect vocal technique denies the singer from performing them properly. Generally, *the composers of these songs and arias were master singers and master vocal teachers themselves.* The *dynamic markings* and *interpretative expressions* inscribed throughout these vocal masterpieces are usually in perfect harmony with the physiological laws of the singing instrument. When observed and respected, they give the singer a most helpful guide for achieving a healthy, consistently well-functioning, superior vocal instrument.

Group 1: *The Sustained Songs*

1. *Amarilli, mia bella*	G. Caccini
2. *Comme raggio di sol*	A. Caldara
3. *Sebben, crudele*	A. Caldara
4. *Vergin, tutto amor*	F. Durante
5. *Caro mio ben*	G. Giordani
6. *O del mio dolce ardor*	C. W. Von Gluck
7. *O cessate di piagarmi*	A. Scarlatti
8. *Tu lo sai*	G. Torelli

Group 2: The Flexible Songs

9. *Per la gloria d'adorarvi*	G. Bononcini
10. *Che fiero costume*	G. Legrenzi
11. *Pur dicesti, o bocca bella*	A. Lotti
12. *Il mio bel foco*	B. Marcello
13. *Nel cor più non mi sento*	G. Paisiello
14. *Se tu m'ami, se sospiri*	G. Pergolesi
15. *Già il sole dal Gange*	A. Scarlatti
16. *Le Violette*	A. Scarlatti

Hearing your own singing voice—can it be actually done?

No singer can hear the quality of her own singing voice with the same reality as others do! The act of singing often seduces the singer into a euphoric state of self-satisfaction in which judgments of vocal standards may be distorted. Therefore, it is wise for singers to periodically ask their teachers, vocal coaches, or someone whose judgment they trust, to tell them *"honestly"* if the tones which they are producing possess beauty, and/or if they are of a potentially professional standard. It is possible for a singer to produce tones that merely seem to be correct and beautiful but are, in reality, unpleasant to listen to. It is up to those who have been asked to judge the singer's voice, to tell her the truth, as they perceive it.

The "inverted" tone

Frequently, a properly focused, *inverted tone,* is described by listeners as being "suspended" and/or "floating". *"Suspended and "floating"* terms are accurate descriptions of a correctly inverted tone because, a floating tone is dominated by an advanced falsetto developed tone, to with the power of the chest voice connected to it, and which is being produced with an ample flow of breath. While an *"inverted tone"* is connected to *"chest voice"* power, it sounds as if it is totally free from any anchor, and that it is "bobbing up and down" and is totally *"disembodied"* from the singer. These descriptions attempt to describe a tone that is almost totally generated by the kinetic energy of the breath flow, and that it possesses *"palatal resonance".*

Despite an "inverted" tone's attachment to chest voice power *(which is necessary for the connected mode of singing),* and to its attachment to its own specific *focal point, which is also necessary, somehow it seems totally "air born" and "totally free".* If such a tone could be actually seen *"it would shimmer continuously, in beauty".* This ideal *"air borne"* tone is the *opposite of* the sort of common-place, *"rigidly gripped", "forced and negatively anchored"* tone, dominated by the negative actions of the chest voice, which is *"immobile" "thick", and "unmusical",* but frequently heard, emanating from most unsuccessful singing students.

An authentic inverted tone is muscularly created by the detached falsetto's u (oo) vowel, and the fullest potential flow of breath being applied to it. By repeatedly "blowing" the fullest potential breath flow into the vowel throat-space of an open-throated, falsetto open u (oo) vowel of a selected tone, it will gradually create the fullest and freest pathway for the breath force to flow into and through this highly developed, open-throated u (oo) vowel, converting its pitch into an *"inverted tone".* After that has been accomplished, the singer should stop using the exaggerated force of the breath stream, with the inverted tone.

After performing many open-throated u (oo) vowel exercises, the voice should be rested for a good while. Afterward, small ascending scales, using the u (oo) vowel should be performed. It is while applying u (oo) vowel scales that the nature of the *"inverted tone"* is revealed to the singer. When this highly desired *"inverted status"* of a tone (s) comes to exist. with all four remaining vowels, they, too, will behave in the same *"free", "puffy", "kinetic",*
"shimmering" manner as an *inverted tone,* as described above.

During the important Paris *voice teaching years* of the great baritone/teacher *Giovanni Sbriglia* and his star pupil, *Jean de Reszke* [3], this critical *"inversion factor"* , which every tone of the student's

---

[3] Giovanni Sbriglia, (1832-1916) outstanding Neapolitan tenor. Debut: San Carlo Theater— 1853. Influential voice teacher in

complete range was made to possess, the tone was said to *"float on a cushion of air"*.

The method of *inverting* all the tones of the singer's vocal range, particularly those of the bottom octave, *is complex in nature* and requires an extended period of time and much practice to understand and accomplish. The singer must take special note that, it is *not* merely an abstract mental *aesthetic* concept, *but rather a tangible, physical accomplishment.* It is also a radical departure from ordinary speech.

To experience the process of "inverting" a selected tone, when applying the remaining vowels, the singer must channel any of the four vowels, other than the u (oo) vowel, through the throat-space of an advanced developed, puffy u (oo) vowel, gradually change it to an o (oh) vowel, then change it again, to any of the selected other four vowels, maintaining strict legato while switching from one vowel to the next. The singer must assure that each vowel, after the initial first u (oo) vowel, is placed in the precise and exact same throat-space of the advanced *"puffy" "kinetic" u (oo) vowel*, while allowing for the difference of each vowel's individual *vowel-throat-space.* Once this has been correctly accomplished, the singer will clearly observe the correct *inverted* throat positions of the remaining vowels, i (ee), e (eh), o (oh) and a (ah), which the starter u (oo) vowel has directed each to, and imposed its *"puffy" (breath),* influence upon it.

At another, different exercise session, start with a detached falsetto o (oh) vowel, and change it slowly to an fully open, brilliant a (ah) vowel, while assuring that a strong current of breath is flowing through the a (ah) vowel. This should clearly reveal to the singer what it means, when it is stated that the a (ah) vowel but never be used unless it has be "mixed" with the head voice's controls. The singer should experiment with all the vowels, pause after each, and make observations judgments about them, too. If the a (ah) vowel communicates to the singer that it is not quite right, then temporarily replace the a (ah) vowel with the *AW* vowel.

The "Vocal Platform"

When the tones of C2 to E2 reach their maximum development, they *and the half tones in-between them,* group themselves extremely closely together. When they are in that close approximation, they create a horizontal *surface (or line),* between the *Bottom Range* and the *Top range.* Through many applications of the *messa di voce,* all these "platform" tones become eventually, *become very strong.* Each of them becomes capable of expanding their volume from *minimum* to *maximum volume,* then being returned to *minimum volume,* and with each of the *five* classic Italian vowels. Knowing *exactly* when they have reached their maximum muscular development has been attained, occurs when a correct, fully open-throated a (ah) vowel can *sung with all of them.* Of course this open throated a (ah) vowel must also be

---

Paris,1875. Jean de Reszke (1850-1925), born in Poland. Principal tenor of the Golden Age of Opera—20th Century. Taught John Charles Thomas, Bidu Sayao, Maggie Teyte, Carmen Melis (who taught Renata Tebaldi), and Clive Carey, who had Joan Sutherland as a student for a period of time.

mixed with the muscular influences of the u (oo) and o (oh) vowels.

The a (ah) vowel automatically brings into play the maximum percentage of *positive chest voice action* to each tone (when the a (ah) is properly mixed). Success with these platform tones, with the a (ah) vowel grants the much desired *"open throat"* vocal production, with all the *Middle Range's* tones that is associated with superior, professional singing, and superior singers.

It is only when the tones situated <u>below</u> — *C♮2, the B♮, B♭, A♮, A♭, G♮, G♭, F♮, E, E♭, D♮ D♭ and middle C—are freed from all chest voice weight and thickness*, that the uniqueness of the Platform's Tones— C♮2 to E♮2—that their true purpose can be clearly understood by the singer. As a group, these five half tones should be thought of as a raised "platform" representing the advanced developed *Middle Range*, which the singer uses as her base of operation, from which she initiates vocal *maneuvers toward the Bottom Range,* when that is called for, *and toward the Top Range,* when that is called for.

The singer must conceive of all the tones located *<u>just below</u> the Vocal Platform,* as her lower range of tones, which must always be sung *softer, in the manner of a sigh, than the tones of all the other areas of her complete range.*

The Platform's tones are capable of very loud dynamic intensities, provided that, when such loud intensity is applied, the tone being sung is accompanied by a full, free flow of the *breath force.* If this is not always adhered to, a platform tone (s) will quickly lose its buoyancy *(the tone flowing on swirling currents of breath)*, and become corrupted by the addition of negative chest voice influence, rising up from the bottom of the ranger and entering into *Vocal Platform.* When more than one of two of the platform's five-half tones is similarly corrupted, the singer may be permanently denied free ascent upward in her range, and denied access to the tones of her *Top Range.*

The *Top Range's* tones *(situated just above the Vocal Platform),* are capable of producing the singer's loudest potential sounds. But understand that this *"loudness factor"* is in no way related to the *loudness potentials* of the *Platform's Tones,* nor the *Bottom Range's* tones. The loudness factor of the *Top Range's tones* is produced, almost exclusively, by a strong collaboration of the *Breath Flow* that is being mixed with the *"brilliant"* vibrations of the vocal cords. The *solidity factor* of these unique top range tones is an illusion, meaning that they *are not mainly* produced by the solid actions of any of the other vocal organs, but instead, almost exclusively by strong, swirling currents of breath. There is a solidity factor, involved in producing superior top tones, and it that, the singer responsible for holding the "walls" of the upper register's resonance cavity *open*, to sustain and absorb the force to the strong current of the breath flow being directed into this particular resonance cavity, by the singer.

To sing the top range's tones correctly, the singer never employs the same physical method of tone production associated with *the middle, or lower throat area.* The best way of discovering the unique blend of swirling breath current and vocal cords' vibrations that produce the Top Range's tones, is through the use of the *detached falsetto voice,* while employing the AW vowel. The AW vowel allows the fullest force of breath to flow, of all the vowels. The singer should perform some sustained, single tone exercises, with the *Top Range's tones*, employing a detached falsetto *AW vowel*, and in some cases the vowel u (oo) vowel, or the o (oh) vowel, by first setting the throat-socket of the selected tone, then blowing exaggerated amounts of breath into it. Then repeat this procedure with several other Top Range Tones. Then the singer should rest her voice for a few hours. When resuming her exploration of the top tones, the singer should put her voice into the "connected mode", wherein the chest and head voice registers are both connected to each other, and sing a few phrases from the *classical songs (p. 106).* It is then that the singer may experience and properly evaluate the benefits which those top tones to which she's applied the exaggerated amounts of breath flow to, have changed.

A simple concept about "voice building" which yields great structural benefits

All vocal progress is primarily dependent upon the correct and full development of the head voice muscles. *Only the fully-developed head voice muscles can, in turn,* alter the behavioral patterns of the chest voice muscles.

The great singer/voice teacher *Giovanni Sbriglia* stated "... everything coordinates always upward, until all the tones seem to *come down* from the resonance cavities of the head."

With this in mind, it is important to present as many image-evoking guidelines as possible to the singer, regarding the various ways in which the developing head voice muscles progress toward their maximum development. Sound judgment about the progressively developing singing voice involves both *the sounds they produce,* interpreted by the singer herself, or by her listeners, *plus the physical sensations* which only the singer can hear.

During past, historic periods of superior vocal training, the process of correctly structuring the singing voice was divided into two main periods:

1) The closed period   —   2) The open period

The "closed (throat)" phase of vocal training

During the *first major phase* of vocal training the singing voice, it is necessary to temporarily neglect the *chest voice muscles* and give *priority* to the development of the head voice muscles. This is mainly accomplished by using the two "closed" *head voice* vowels, u (oo) and i (ee), for most of the beginning exercises. In the very beginning, employ the u (oo) vowel, more frequently than the i (ee) vowel. With the ongoing applications of these two head voice vowels, in conjunction with the descending falsetto scales, and the swelled-tone exercise, *which should be applied later on, in the first phase of training,* the singer begins to sense a gradual and continual "closing down" of her voice. The "wide open" throat-sockets and easy outpouring of volume generally granted to most beginners, by the *incorrect use of the "raw" chest voice, while employing* the "open" a (ah) vowel, gradually vanishes. These wide-open, "raw" tones are gradually replaced by *"developing tones"* of limited volume and *"closed"* throat-sockets. *These are all correct muscular responses of the developing falsetto, appropriate to the "1ˢᵗ closed throat phase" of vocal development.*

This does not imply that during the 1ˢᵗ phase of development the singer is completely denied vocal power, but whatever power is available, it becomes involuntarily narrowed, in its "path of projection" through the throat and the full length of the resonance channel. Because of this, muscular harmony between the two registers is temporarily denied, and the singer is subject to frequent vocal *"shut downs"*. Despite these discouraging factors, the singer must persist with the closed vowels u (oo) and i (ee), and the swelled-tone exercises. They must be used until the muscles of the falsetto tones develop sufficient strength to completely transfer the power of the chest voice through the "closed" throat-spaces of all tones from C2 upward, to the top of the range. The singer must oscillate her practice sessions between using her singing voice in its *detached falsetto form*, then, at other times in its *"connected form"*, appropriately for actually singing and performing.

By utilizing the oscillating pattern of exercising her voice, switching back and forth between the *connected mode* and the *detached mode,* the singer may monitor and judge all progressive vocal improvements, in all areas of her complete range.

At some point, during a performance the swelled-tone exercises, the singer will be able to increase the volume of the tone being presently exercised to the point where the brilliant, vibrant power of the chest voice harmoniously unites itself with the detached, falsetto controlled starter-tone. When this occurs with the e (eh) vowel, it signifies that the closed, detached falsetto tones, *which must be used for a long time,* are now ready *"to open"*. This leads to more successes with the swelled-tone exercise, and possibly with the two "open vowels", the o (oh) and the (ah). *When the singer can successfully perform a series of complete swelled-tone exercises, with each of the five vowels u (oo), i (ee), e (eh), o (oh) and a (ah), the accomplishment brings the singing instrument to the "open phase" of her vocal training. Arriving at the new "open phase" is seldom quickly.*

The "mixed voice" or "mezzo-falso" voice

It is about this time, in the vocal structural program, that a new vocal control presents itself to the singer. The new muscular control is called the *mixed voice*, or as it was named by the old Italian teachers, the *"mezzo-falso"* voce. Which is the very factor that aids the singer to make her transition from the *1ˢᵗ "closed phase"* of her vocal training, to the new, and *uncharted 2ⁿᵈ phase* of her vocal development.

As the muscles of the falsetto or *"whistle voice"*, located in her *Top Range,* grow very strong, through repeated performances of the swelled-tone exercise, it begins to become rather easily performed.

These *"whistle voice"* tones become strong enough to *allow the singer to thread all of the power of the chest voice through the falsetto starter-tone,* while performing the *messa di voce* and the *"mixed voice" is born.* Now, with possession of the newly arrived *"mixed voice"* the singer gains a muscular mechanism for controlling the actions of both the registers which allows her to completely join both registers harmoniously together, on any given tone, and at any place in of her complete range.

　　Note that: Hence forth, we shall referred to the mezzo falso, by it more popular name "the mixed voice".

　　While the swelled-tone exercises have finally mollified the "raw" energy of the chest voice, they have simultaneously strengthened the muscles of the falsetto voice to such a point that it changes greatly, both in its sound qualities and basic muscular responses. All the falsetto's tones begin to lose their *"false and unnatural sounds".* It may be pleasant to recall now that, at the beginning of vocal structuring, these wrongly judged *"false and unnatural"* qualities had denied the singer, *and her listeners,* from making accurate judgments of what the falsetto tones could eventually become, when properly development.

　　Now, these advanced, fully-developed falsetto tones begin to sound *like miniature versions of the chest voice tones,* while still retaining the muscular integrity of their original, falsetto controls *(now advanced greatly in development),* and a most important factor to keep in mind, they have retained their original falsetto *"sweetness"* and *"youthful"* qualities.

　　With advanced development, the *falsetto range* can now be extended both *upward* and *downward* in the range, and made to influence the tones of those regions. However, their flexibility becomes temporarily limited, because they have been brought into close approximation with the throat-sockets of all the chest voice tones *(the result of the swelled-tone exercise),* and their accompanying increase in weight.

　　The *mixed voice should not* be confused with *mezza-voce* singing, since *mezza-voce singing* means singing with the "half voice" or with diminished volume. No singer can quickly come to possess the *mixed voice,* since it does not appear until the swelled-tone exercises have been applied to the detached falsetto tones for a long period of time. When the *mixed voice* mechanism does become available, on every tone of the singer's range *(and most critically, with the lower notes),* the singer may observe that it automatically alters the participation of the chest voice's action, with all tones of a particular vocal exercise, or operatic phrase, and when ascending the range. It reduces all the chest voice's negative bulk and weight with them, permitting only a minimal percentage of the chest voice's dynamic potential to be transported upward along the vocal tract. Each tone of a rising scale should be started with the mixed voice's mechanism of control, and only afterwards should the vibrant power of the chest voice be brought into full play.

　　Although the *mixed voice* enables the uniting of the two registers, the registers still remain separate entities, apart from each other. Although they are capable of simultaneously interacting with each other, the two highly developed registers also remain capable of functioning separately and individually from each other. The *detached falsetto,* too, remains a separate entity, possessing the capability of being detached from the chest voice. During the *50s* some of the older teacher of the Italian school referred to the mixed voice as *"the third register."*

Since the *mixed voice* and the *detached falsetto* always retain an option to be separated from each other, they can therefore be employed separately, or in unison. When the *detached falsetto* grows in strength to the point that it *"invites" (on its own),* the actions of the *mixed voice,* there remains a subtle difference between the two. If there is confusion about making an accurate distinction between the two, as to which is which, the singer should direct her attention to the different percentages of *breath support* demanded, to produce each of them. The *detached falsetto* requires *practically no breath support,* whereas the *mixed voice requires much more breath support,* by comparison; it demands almost as much as when the *full chest power* has been added to any given tone. Only the singer *(or a truly qualified voice teacher),* can distinguish the differences of sound between the two mechanisms of control, the *"detached falsetto"* and the *"mixed voice".* This is because, in their advanced stage of development, they both sound very much alike.

The *"Witch's Voice", or the "voce di strega"*

One of the unusual, transitory phases which the *falsetto voice* goes through, on its way to becoming the *mixed voice* is called the *"witch's voice",* so named because of its harsh, strident, unmusical sounds. The *witch's voice* should be welcomed by the singer, as it often signals *the end* of the *"closed phase"* of vocal training, and *the beginning* of the *"open phase".* When the *witch's tones* first arrive they *sound loud, harsh, and edgy,* and are of an *unprofessional standard.* In this early, "raw" state, they should be thought of positively, and as being the *precursors* of the great *squillo* tones, of a great singer. The Italian term *squillo* means *"to blare"* or *"ring out."* *Squillo* tones *"skyrocket"* over the orchestra, outward into the theater. Only those singers who have completely subjugated the power of the chest voice's force, and transformed its tones into the *precise weight* and appropriate *throat-shapes* that may be fitted precisely *into the inherently narrow contours of the upper head voice tract,* are privileged to possess *squillo* tones.

The *"open throated"* phase

These *squillo* tones are most compatibly with the i (ee) and e (eh) vowels. But with advanced vocal structuring, tones using the o (oh) and a (ah) vowels may come to possess the *"ringing and projecting"* qualities and attributes of the *witch voice.* For example, the a (ah) vowel's *"witch voice"* phase of development may be identified by the sound of such words as *at, hat, pat, sat, mat,* etc., sounds which are often referred to as "the Boston *ah*".

When this "raw" and *"extremely open" at word's* sound becomes available to the singer it possesses the ability to stretch her throat-position of a selected tone, to a position of maximum "openness." But this "openness" has its limitations, which will be explained. The "raw" and "spread" *at sound,* has a potential for helping the singer achieve superior, well rounded a (ah) vowels, especially with her high notes. The *at word's* sound may be gradually altered and refined by adjusting its throat-space toward a rounded o (oh) vowel's throat-position, while adding a tint of the u (oo) vowel to the selected tone. The u (oo) and o (oh), vowels' positive influences will alter the tone's *rawness* and transform it towards an improved state of *"roundness"* and *"mellowness".*

The sounds of the *witch's voice* are *parented* by many successful, swelled-tone exercises employing an open, breathy i (ee) vowel, which has been passed through the *open throated-space* of a fully open a (ah) vowel. Sopranos, passing through this unusual, *temporary phase* of vocal development, can best produce the *"witch's cackle"* with her *upper middle pitches*, from E♮ to B♮, above C2, by emitting a series of *"hee-hee-hee"* sounds, imitating an old, female witch. After a certain time, the rawness of the *witch voice* must be put aside. As the *"witch voice"* develops further, its raw sounds gradually mellow and become totally transformed from *"ugly and undesirable",* into tones of superior quality, and of course, they also possess "projecting power."

The "narrow beams of sound" of the upper range

When a correctly trained singer sings a phrase that rises toward her *Top Range,* there occurs incremental increases of volume accompanying it. However, the singer perceives this increase in volume very differently than do her listeners. The singer's listeners, hearing one of the singer's sustained *Top Range's tones,* perceives it as being a wide, voluminous spray of beautiful vocal sound. But the singer, herself, perceives this same sustained *Top Range* tone as a very soft tone, with a limited "width ". This is so because the singer *is not* privileged to hear her voice with the same reality as others do.

This discrepancy of perception between what *the singer feels and hears* and *what her listeners hear,* has a physiological explanation. When sustaining one of her *Top Range's* tones, the singer may erroneously desire to transport the *full width* of her the chest voice upward, to that particular high note, but if her voice has been properly structured, she *will not* be permitted to do so. This is so because her *Top Range's tones* have been subjected to superior structuring principles. These vocal exercises of these principles have greatly strengthened the muscular contours of her Top Range's tones, while allowing them to retain their inherent, *thin and narrow muscular* forms. Because of that, whenever this fortunate singer sends an ascending phrase whizzing toward her Top Range, all the pitches of that vocal phrase, *riding on strong current of the breath force,* arrive at F♮2, where they unavoidably encounter the thin, narrow muscular contours of Top Range, which forces her avoid thickening them, and to instead *narrow* them, which simultaneously reduces their undesirable *mass and bulk.*

When most contemporary singers sing a phrase which mounts to the *Top Range* of their voices, they erroneously and intentionally attempt to negatively widen their Top Range's tones' throat-positions, basing their actions upon a misguided training-principle, concerning the *Top Range's tones*, which instructs the singer to *"open up"* the throat-sockets of all their *Top Range's* tones, to their maximum potential. As a consequence of doing that, all the tones of the rising phase, upon first arriving at the entrance to the Top Range, "slam up" against the thinner and narrower muscular contours of their *Top Range* are blocked and denied further ascent. When this be the case, some singer, with limited head voice development, manager to keep the rinsing scale ascending, but "small", "pinched" tones of limited volume, poor quality, that lack ringing core brilliance, and focus. Consequently their *"unfulfilled top tones"* are usually overpowered by the orchestra.

The most critical factors missing, with most contemporary singing voices, are:

1) In their *Top Range,* the full and correct addition of the chest voice power, in its transformed state, meaning when it has been "mixed", and made to *operate in collaboration with the muscular controls of the head voice.*

2) The *Lower Range* of most contemporary singers are negatively dominated by the rigid and inflexible *Chest Voice's* negative muscular influences, *whereas these Lower Register's tones should be dominated by the flexible, malleable, muscular controls of the Head Voice,* which allows the singer to sing with beauty of tone and *cantilena. Cantilena* is an artistic manner of singing softly, especially in the *bottom range,* in the manner of a whisper, that can easily be heard at the rear of the theater. Or, conversely, these same lower tones can be sung as loudly as a *"cultivated shout",* as Jean de Reszke was *fond of saying, when he wished to describe opera singing, to one of his new pupils.*

Cantilena gives superior singing the illusion of *"regular speech"* patterns, but it is so *distant* from regular speech, as to be totally unimaginable by today's average vocal student. When a singer possess the skill and muscular controls of *cantilena,* she is privileged to create a large variety of tonal colors, while clearly *"pronouncing"* the words being sung, with clarity and authenticity, all of which gives the dramatic moment a sense of truth and vitality. All the great *"singing-actresses"* of the past possessed a *flawless cantilena.*

More about the " gathered" voice

When the power of the chest voice has been correctly united to the advanced falsetto voice in the *Middle Range*—C2 to the E2 above it—through the use of the *mixed voice,* all the *Middle Range tones* gathered themselves closely together, so that all their muscular controls become highly manageable by the singer, as if they were but one, single pitch. This allows the singer to regulate the various percentages of the breath dynamics that must be applied to them, from the softest of volume, to the loudest of volume, *and then to return the selected tone to a ppp dynamic. But more importantly, the "gathered voice"* allows the singer to control and reduce the broad movements of the muscles of her tongue, lips, and cheeks, which are very involved in producing the five classic Italian vowels, plus the consonants *to a minimum.* The singer accomplishes this by isolating the muscles which control the production of *basic tone and* vowel, *from those muscles that produce the consonants.*

The *mixed voice* helps the singer to accomplish all the above, because the mixed voice is capable of *compressing and reducing* the pressure of the breath force, that is focused upon any selected tone. While singing, the head voice's muscles, operating in rear, *upper throat region of the mouth-pharynx cavity,* manage the production of the pitch and vowel, *while the tip of the tongue and cheeks operating in the frontal region of the mouth,* manage the consonants—all, in "split seconds", moments before the singer launches the tone that she's about to be sing, outward to her audience. Acquiring the muscular abilities and skills of using the *mixed voice,* and the mental know-how to accomplish all the above tasks, takes a long time. But, when the singer can successfully pull it all off—beauty of tone, purity of vowel, precise intonation, and clarity of pronunciation abound! Well! It's no wonder that we presently have *no Zinka Milanovs,* no *Tebaldis,* no *Rethbergs,* no *Flagstads,* no *Caballés,* no *Giglis,* no *Bjöerlings,* no *Warrens,* no *Simionatos,* no *Pinzas,* and so-on-and-so fort, since the old, tried and proven *classic school of voice training has long been gone and forgotten.*

The great singing teachers of the past called the many capabilities of the *mixed voice—la voce racolta—*meaning *"the Gathered Voice" or "The voice of the Throat."*

"The voice of the throat"

We have established that, when all the tones of the *upper passaggio, as well as those of the lower, true passaggio* reach an advanced stage of development they all *"gather"* closely together. And, beside the wonders of the *mixed voice,* these closely gathered tones grant the singer another important singing tool, *la voce di gola,* meaning the *"voice of the throat".* This *voce di gola* is, in actuality, a series of several or more nerve, information-communication responses, which occur in the upper, posterior area of the mouth-pharynx cavity, while the singing is actually singing, and which grant the singer a miniature, preview version of the forthcoming tone, mere seconds before she will launch it outward to her audience, so that she can quickly alter any factors which she interprets to be negative, or conversely, she can quickly give the tone in question her full approval, if it meets all her high standards, then send it on its way.

All the master-teachers of the past agreed that, *"unless a singer is capable of silently and inwardly hearing the correctness or incorrectness of a given tone, seconds before she is about to deliver it to her listeners, she would never be able to sing consistently with superior tone."* This means that the *voce di gola* is capable of informing the singer, seconds before she is about to sing a selected tone, whether all the technical requirements—*"vowel placement", "the proper amount of breath force", "accurate focal-point direction"*, *"tongue, lips, cheeks adjustments"*, *etc.*, are correct, or incorrect.

Only when all the muscles of the vocal instrument have reached their maximum development will the singer come to possess this extraordinary *voce di gola.*

It was often said, by superior singers of the past, that they *"listen for"* and *"pre-hear"* the precise tone they intend to produce, split seconds before actually singing it. In the pass, that was frequently possible, because, during the long period of voice building, which the singer had passed through, the brain had retained many *"memories"* of the various ways in which the correct structuring process gradually took place, and had stored them all in the student's brain, so that in the future, when she became a professional singer, all these important technical factors could be *flashed back* into her conscious awareness, and aid her to make all important technical judgments about a selected tone, which she was about to launch outward to her audience.

Present-day singers may scoff in disbelief at the above information. But when most of *them* are about to deliver a vocal phrase to their audience, it seems that their only guide for producing it, is to immediately call into play all the incorrect *frontal muscular controls of the speaking voice*, which are invalid factors for the correct use of the singing voice, and which repeatedly produce mediocrity and frequently failure.

CHAPTER SIX

"Low larynx" position versus *"high larynx" position*

There exists a long standing debate as to whether the singer should maintain a "low larynx" position or a "high larynx" position while singing. The larynx should never be made to remain in any one rigidly fixed position. It must be allowed full flexibility of movement.

There are *two major modes* of using the singing instrument, and the larynx behaves differently in each. The *1st* is the *exercise mode*, and the *2nd* is the *singing mode*. When the voice is in *exercise mode*, the position of the larynx should be given full, free range of movement. It can then respond appropriately to the progressive positionings which each of the five instrumental vowels, individually exert upon its singing position, and also submit to the influences of the pitch being presently sung.

When in *exercise mode, as when using the detached falsetto*, the hollow u (oo) vowel is best for correctly positioning the larynx, since it *does not* employ the power of the chest voice. Upon connecting any of the remaining four vowels—i (ee), e (eh), o (oh), and a (ah)—to the hollow u (oo) vowel, the singer is undeniably obliged to switch to the *connected mode* and to *"clamp"* the power of the *chest voice* to the starter-tone being sung. Each individual vowel will then, respectively, effect the positioning of the larynx.

Of these four vowels *(other than the u (oo)*, the open, detached falsetto i (ee), applied in a *descending direction, downward from the Top Range,* will allow *only the precise amount of chest voice participation*, while correctly positioning the larynx appropriately, and relative to the pitch and vowel being presently sung. Therefore the remaining vowels e (eh), o (oh), and a (ah), where the correct positions of the larynx are concerned, can be tuned by the detached falsetto, open i (ee) vowel when the detached falsetto's i (ee) vowel's throat position is based upon the hollow u (oo) vowel.

When exercising the open i (ee) vowel with the falsetto voice, there are many times when *it pulls the larynx to an abnormally high position.* These abnormally high positions are *only temporary* and they must be allowed. They permit the tone being exercised to locate its precise *focal point* along the full length of the entire *resonance channel.* As a consequence, the larynx position of each tone and vowel will automatically adjust to the proper height/and or depth, without straying form its correct focal point, which the open i (ee) vowel exercise has precisely identified for it. It is always advisable to rest the voice for a few hours, or even a day, after employing the detached, falsetto open i (ee) vowel. Upon returning to the next exercises session, the singer should perform a few simple scales in the *Lower Range,* using the AW vowel, or o (oh) vowel, but now, exclude the use of the i (ee) and e (eh) vowels, then afterwards, sing some of the classical songs *(pg. 106).*

When the singer performs a simple ascending scale, using the open AW vowel, in the *connected mode, and generating a full free flow of the breath stream*, the position of the larynx lowers away from the extremely high position, created by the detached falsetto open i (ee) vowel, and reveals the precise "performance position" or *focal point* for the larynx, for each individual pitch of the scale. Performing the same simple ascending scales with the open e (eh), open o (oh), and open a (ah) vowels further alters the position of the larynx, each respective to the individual vowel being presently sung's particular effect upon it. The singer should carefully observe the various responses of the larynx which each individual vowel evokes. However, while performing these scales, the larynx's position must remain flexible, so it can readily respond and adjust to the next tone and its accompanying vowel, since each higher *(or lower)*, note requires a slightly different *laryngo-pharnygeal* adjustment.

The most critical movement which the larynx makes is one that *the singer is obliged to consciously make, for herself.* Otherwise, the *breath force will not* be able to flow along the complete resonance channel, into the appropriate resonance cavity, for the tone. When the singer has not sung for a period of time, and warms up the singing voice, she must *consciously* move her larynx from its resting position, which is rather low in the throat channel, and reposition it against the first tone of the vocal platform—C2. This is best accomplished by employing a soft, open-throated *u (oo),* or an *o (oh)* vowel, both of which will help her lift the larynx from its lower resting position and attach it to the C2 tone. Then she must proceed to swell the E♮2 tone to a *mf* dynamic in order to add the action of the chest voice to it, then, using a descending direction, do the same with the E♭2, D♮2, D♭2, and C♮2. When this has been accomplished, the larynx will have been moved to its proper *Middle Range* positions, and as the *"warms up"* progresses, then the singer moves on to either the tones of the *Lower Range*, or the tone of the *Top Range*, where upon, even more adjustments of the larynx and pharynx to each other will occur.

These necessary repositioning of the larynx are only possible for a singer who has reduced the negative bulk of the chest voice, in her *Bottom Range*, by completely overlapping all its tones with the muscular controls of the upper register. Then afterward, perfecting the *messa di voce* exercise with all of these lower tones, using all vowels. At first, these new, higher positions of the larynx may seem to be a great distance from their *"old familiar position"*. In reality, they are a very short distance. When correctly accomplished, these adjustments of the larynx make accessible to the singer the resonating cavities of the mouth-pharynx and head, where vocal resonance occurs. And, it clarifies to her the *precise focal point* of each tone located in her *Middle Range, and the range just above it,* and also, the focal points of her *Top Range*. Many successful singers have described these adjustments of the larynx as "...attaching their larynx to their soft palate". [4]

At one time in the past, the resonance factor of these *"middle range"* tones was referred to as possessing *"palatal"* resonance. This was because these singers knew how to project the breath force into

----

[4] "All beauty in the art of song in the *cantilena,* as well as in all technique, rests chiefly in uninterrupted connection between the soft palate with the hard palate, in the continually elastic adjustment of the former to the latter." Lilli Lehmann.

their *Middle Range,* and they acutely felt the vibrations of these *platform tones* in the region of their soft palates, when the soft palate was positioned, as when gargling with mouthwash, to cleanse the mouth and throat. Earlier in training, when the singer could only sing these *middle range, platform tones* with the *underdeveloped falsetto voice,* in the disconnected mode, the quality of these tones was referred to as "opaque" and/or "covered". This limitation would not allow the singer to add the core brilliance of the chest voice to these tones, especially with the difficult, fully open a (ah) vowel. When the core brilliance of the chest voice finally became available, the quality of these middle range tones were then referred to as *"brilliant" and more importantly, "open".* In the past, the old master-teachers described this accomplishment as *"...piercing the soft palate"* with the *"brilliance"* of the chest voice.

The initial task of repositioning the larynx, with each individual pitch of the complete singing range, with the help of the swelled-tone exercise and the *open-throated, detached falsetto i (ee) vowel* takes a long time. This is because, at the onset of training, the larynx is often found to be long-time mired in a rigid, inflexible position, somewhere in the lower throat channel. This is the result of having performed many incorrectly applied ascending scales that force the "raw" chest voice, employing a (ah) vowel, upward into the platform's tones. However, after all the correct larynx positionings have been accomplished, warming up the voice can be accomplished in just a few minutes.

While repositioning the larynx, during the vocal warm-up, the singer *must not* allow the larynx to position itself on any of the tones below the vocal platform—C2 for all sopranos. Otherwise, the "entrance" into the upward curving resonance channel, leading through the registers' break and to the tones of the Top Range, would remain closed to the flow of the breath stream. The singer must carefully guide her larynx, upward in the rear of the mouth cavity, toward the first pitch of the vocal platform, which is C2. Employing a hollow u (oo) vowel, she must then gently, but firmly clamp the u (oo) vowel, then larynx there, *(by breath pressure),* prolong it for a few moments, then change the u (oo) to an open i (ee) vowel, then swell the tone to add the chest voice power.

When this specific placement of the larynx has been accomplished, the singer may use both the *upward pulls* of the head voice muscles, *evoked by the use of the u (oo) and i (ee) vowels.*

The singer will come to learn that this critical "first" C2 pitch of the vocal platform, does not readily submit to her intention of positioning and "clamping" the larynx to it. This is because it is inherently weak and disadvantageously located in close proximity to the stronger muscles of the chest voice. The tones of the *chest voice range* persistently act as rivals to the *Middle Range,* tending always to claim this C2 for its own. But with persistence, this *"first"* platform tone can be made strong enough to detach itself from the negative influence of the chest voice's "downward pull", and accept the correct, higher positioning of the larynx upon it, by the muscular controls of the head voice. Once the singer has succeeded with the *detached falsetto,* open i (ee) vowel on the first platform tone, the open e (eh), open o (oh), and open a (ah) vowels must also be won over to success, through the swelled-tone exercise, and with all the remaining pitches of the *vocal platform.*

Francesco Lamperti, one of the most eminent teachers of the post-*Bel Canto* period, identified C2 to be "... the *most* difficult tone in the entire vocal range with which to perfect the *messa di voce* exercise, and with all five vowels".

The reason that *the larynx must be repositioned* from its lower resting place, upon the first tone of the vocal platform, is so the negative factors of the chest voice will , which immediate cause vocal rigidity, not be permitted to rise upward in the range and *block the Breath Stream* from flowing freely through the *upper passaggio,* and further upward into the *Top Range.*

William Shakespeare, a famous concert and oratorio tenor, teacher of singing, and one of *Francesco Lamperti's* most eminent students, wrote a well-known treatise on singing in *1921* entitled *The Art of Singing.*[5] In it he states, "... in order to produce any note in fullness and purity of tone, it is necessary to place or balance the larynx over the breath and retain its appropriate position there, *while singing.* This involves the upward, forward or backward pulling muscles upon the tongue-bone, *the hyoid bone,* balanced by those muscles *pulling the vocal instrument downwards towards the chest bone* ."

Frequently, present-day teachers mistakenly instruct their students to place and maintain their larynx in a *"low position"* at the very bottom of their vocal range. This results in the student singing rigid, thick, one-dimensional tones. This mistaken method is often applied to achieve quick results in obtaining *"resonant, professional quality tones."* Most singers who use the *"fixed, low larynx position method"* eventually learn that it is short-lived, because it excludes the participation of the upper register's muscular actions in all tone production. These abnormally *"dark", "thick", "forced resonance"* sounds are produced by a rigid jaw and "low larynx" position, which causes many voices to be incorrectly classified into a lower, and inappropriate vocal category. One symptom of the *"lower, rigid larynx position's" incorrectness* is revealed when singers employing it cannot sing a pure u (oo) vowel, nor a pure i (ee) vowel. Their impure u (oo) vowel distorts toward the sound of *"uh" or "oh",* or even *(ah),* and their impure i (ee) vowel distorts toward a wide, *inappropriate e (eh) vowel.*

After the voice has reached an advanced state of vocal development, there comes into existence *three separate and distinct muscular mechanisms for controlling all the tones of the complete vocal range.* These *three separate muscular mechanisms* are physically located in very close, parallel proximity to each other, along the entire length of the *resonance channel.* These mechanisms *can not* be correctly evoked and employed at the beginning of vocal training, but come gradually into use with the creation of the resonance channel, itself. Each of these three mechanisms has its own distinct muscular actions and tonal qualities, and each relates to any given tone, in proportion *to the depth or percentage of the vocal cords' participation* of the tone.

    1) The *"detached falsetto"* serves as the "starter" of all tone (s):

    2) The *mixed voice,* when subjected to an increase of breath pressure, brings into play an

---

[5] *The Art of Singing,* William Shakespeare, Ditson, New York, 1921.

increase of depth of the vocal cords' participation. This *mixed voice* mechanism controls the addition or subtraction of the chest voice's power, accomplished by swelling or diminishing the volume of the detached falsetto "starter-tone";

    3) The *"connected"* mode of the two registers is called the *"full voice"*, a translation of the Italian term *la voce piena.* When the full voice is operative, there exists *a maximum connection* of *the chest voice's muscular controls* to the *muscular controls of the advanced developed falsetto* with every tone of the complete range. The *full voice* automatically gives any tone its "real sound", *as opposed to the "false" sound which the early face of the detached falsetto gives to any tone*, or, the readily recognizable *"performing quality"* of the voice. When we say that the *full voice* requires a maximum connection of the chest voice's power, we *do not* imply that the singer must produce the voice's *maximum power.* We mean merely that, all the various potential uses of the singing voice *can not* be made available until the muscular controls of both the chest voice and head voice have been put into maximum, harmonious connection to each other.

The three separate muscular mechanism that control the advanced developed voice:

    1. The detached falsetto—
    2. The mixed voice—
    3. The full voice—

Structurally speaking, it must be remembered that, for all three of these precious mechanisms, the long and tedious *developmental process* has precise, sequential order of development which must be rigidly maintained, and they are:

    A) All primary vocal exercises must be aimed at first developing the *detached falsetto*, which in time, reaches an advanced stage of its development, and brings into existence—
    B) The *mixed voice,* which when achieved, automatically grants the singer control over—
    C) The addition or subtraction of the chest voice power, *or the "full voice",* to all the tones of the complete range, *which is the only mode of the two vocal registers that will allow the singer to professionally perform.*

Figure 1

An abstract representation of the three
vocal mechanisms of control when they
are separated into layers.

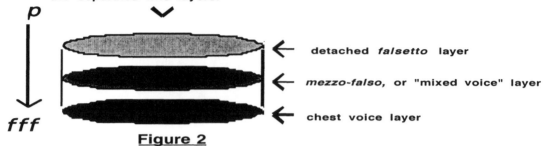

p

fff

← detached *falsetto* layer

← *mezzo-falso*, or "mixed voice" layer

← chest voice layer

Figure 2

An abstract representation of the three
vocal mechanisms of control when they are
"gathered" and brought closely   together.

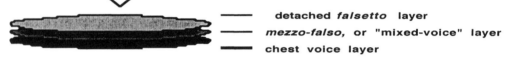

detached *falsetto* layer

mezzo-falso, or "mixed-voice" layer

chest voice layer

When these three mechanisms are used in unison they give the
singer the full voice or "performing voice"

No other order of sequential, progressive development will achieve for the singer the possession of these three individual and separate muscular controls of the singing instrument. Those singers whose training methods do not follow this precise developmental order can only attain *incomplete aspects* of these muscular controls. This is because, some or many of the tones of their singing range will not have been developed from the *purest starting point* of the detached falsetto. Most contemporary singers eagerly seek alternative, inadequate ways of training their singing voices which forces the two vocal registers into a compromised relationship with each other. When that be the case, the most significant structural factor that is lacking is the singer's inability to start a tone with a pianissimo dynamic, increase its volume to a fortissimo, then without stopping to take a new breath, return to the original pianissimo tone. Consequentially, wrongly aligned vocal registers leave the singing voice forever "muffled" with little variety of tonal colors, and no control of the breath force dynamics, whatsoever! And, there is never a tone sung *(especially in the high range),* that starts with a "thread of voice" *(una fil di voce)*, which is swelled to full volume, a vocal maneuver that is thrilling to the listener.

The only way a singer can fully understand the basic, individual nature and functions of the *detached falsetto voice,* the *mixed voice*, and the *full voice* is for her to perfect the *messa di voce* exercise with each and every tone of her complete vocal range. Here are precise guidelines for performing a correct *messa di voce:*

1) The *messa di voce* exercise must begin with a very soft, *detached falsetto tone* that has *no involvement* with the power of the chest voice.

2) The singer swells the volume of a selected tone, by increasing the amount of breath pressure applied to it, which gradually increases the percentage or *"depth" of participation of the vocal cords.* At the same time, the swelling process brings the tone to a new point where the *mixed voice* mechanism of control becomes available.

3) The singer continues swelling the volume of the tone, which demands a *still greater percentage of vocal cords "depth" of participation.* Simultaneously, the mixed voice has completely pulled the solidity of the chest voice up to the *starter-tone*, while guiding the solidity factor, to its precise throat-socket or *focal point.* The tone is then in a state of *"full voice connection".*

Once the singer has arrived at *Phase 3* of the swelled-tone exercise, she possesses the option to remain at a *medium dynamic, or bring the tone to its fullest projecting power.* Varying the volume of any tone alters its *"vowel color".* Varying the volume of a tone gives the singing voice a variety of interesting vocal colors which hold her listeners' interest. When considering any tone's full range of potential dynamics, each dynamic level can be related to one of these three phases of the swelling-process:

With Phase 1, the singer can produce a tone of the softest volume and texture, *but one that still remains falsetto oriented.* However, after the singer has brought the tone to *Phase 2,* she can clamp the power of the chest voice to the starter-tone, by using the *mixed voice* mechanism of control, and then sing a *true pianissimo* of ethereal beauty. The soft tone of *Phase 1* differs from the soft tone of *Phase 2* in that, the addition of the chest voice's contributions adds to the tone the chest voice's "core brilliance", even at a *pianissimo* dynamic level, which it would not otherwise possess.

After accomplishing *Phases 1 and 2,* the singer has "clamped" the muscular controls of the *detached falsetto* to the muscular controls of the *chest voice,* but has *not yet* attached it *to the fullest percentage of the chest voice's power.*

At *Phase 2,* the singer possesses the option to pass beyond the *pianissimo,* to a *mezzo-forte dynamic.* Once in *Phase 2,* she becomes aware that there is and urgent need for a *greater amount of breath tension, than was required by Phase 1.* This increase of breath tension is necessary because the tone is now supporting more of the chest voice's weight.

When the singer has arrived at *Phase 3,* an additional application of *still greater breath tension is required* to maintain the vitality and precise intonation of the tone. *Phase 3 enables the singer to add the full power of the chest voice to the tone.* But, employing full power could have a potential negative effect, if the singer is not able to diminish the tone back again, to the same softer volume that it possessed in *Phase 2.* When continuing to diminish the tone further, the singer must be able to reduce the volume back to what it was in *Phase 1, meaning,* back to a *detached falsetto controlled tone, as it was operating, at the beginning of the exercise.*

The "puffy" throat sensations of the advanced falsetto tones

After the falsetto muscles have passed through the aforementioned, advanced developmental phases and the singer can consistently perform a correct swelled-tone exercise, the *detached falsetto voice (which must forever be maintained),* generally undergoes many radical changes, both in sound and action. Firstly, each detached falsetto tone becomes so greatly reduced in volume that the singer can only achieve its required detachment status, by singing with minimal volume, resulting in a tone that is merely a whisper, but still possesses a great deal of strength. The opening of the presently sung tone, at the back of the throat, also narrows, greatly. These new, soft, detached falsetto tones, *which produce vowel sounds that are very similar to full volume sounds, and they* are extremely musical and beauty, and they are accompanied by *"puffy"* throat sensations. These *puffy* sensations are positive indications that the muscles of both registers are finally completely cooperate with each other, and are being predominantly produces by strong currents of the breath force, and grant to the singer all the beneficial factors and muscular controls of both registers.

The limited, soft dynamics of the *advanced developed*, detached falsetto tones is a physical reality imposed upon all tones of the singer's range, resulting in their loud dynamic now being *permanently denied.* Any performance of the swelled-tone exercise has become easy and "second-natured." The three separate mechanisms of control—*the detached falsetto*, the *mixed voice*, and the *full voice*, become so closely *"gathered"* together, that all the singers tones now possess an *"impacted"* quality. Each tone of the complete range possesses a full spectrum of superior muscular actions and qualities—*softness, loudness, sweetness, power, darkness, brightness*, and a *"diamond-like"* core brilliance.

This advanced state of the *voce racolta* or *"gathered voice"* may present difficulties for the singer, in evoking and preserving each pitch of the complete range's required *"detached status"* from the full, or performing voice. Any *"connected tone"*, meaning *when both registers are operating together,* must be capable of freeing itself from its chest voice connection and once again become a detached falsetto tone. This is critically important, so that the singer can gradually add the power of the chest voice in incremental percentages, and at his own pace. It can be confusing for the singer to evoke the detached falsetto, after all tones of the range have reached the advanced state of the "gathered voice". This is because, when all three mechanisms of control—the *detached falsetto*, the *mixed voice,* and the *full voice*—reach an advanced level of muscular development and harmony with each other, they prefer to remain "grouped" in close physical proximity to each other, rather than be separated into individual "layers". But separated they must be, to permit the singer a "fresh" correct warm-up, for each new day's singing. If the singer insists that her first, starter-tone of her warm-up begins softly, and she feels the "puffy throat sensations" of the breath flowing freely into it, then she will know that the detached falsetto has been properly evoked and she may add the other two levels of vocal intensity to the selected tone, and that her warm-up session will turn out successfully.

These *"shimmering, puffy, falsetto vibrations"* felt in all the resonator cavities, on a selected pitch, are in perfect harmony with a corresponding, exact pitch of the chest voice system, below it. This harmony communicates to the singer the precise path of ascent which the chest power vibrations must take along the resonance channel, in order to arrive at its terminal *"hook up"* point appropriately for the tone being presently sung, and within its appropriate resonance cavity. It is these "puffy" sensations that give the singer a clear understanding of how the positive *though often "raw"* power of the chest voice can be incorporated into the puffy sensations of the detached falsetto tone, with the help of the *mixed voice*, and produce a superior tone which is smooth, beautiful powerful and highly controllable.

The great Italian tenor/ master teacher *Antonio Sbriglia (1832-1916)*, and the voice teacher of Jean de Reszke, utilized these tiny *"puffy"*, advanced falsetto tones to identify and develop the *head voice* of all his female students. *Giovanni Sbriglia* also used his *"falsettini"* tones to develop the Top Range of his male students. Some individuals *do not* believe that the female voice possesses a falsetto register, *but it does,* and it is called the *"whistle voice"*. *Sbriglia's* tiny u (oo) vowel tones, *sung with the detached falsetto, with a ppp dynamic,* serve the singer well, to make a precise distinction between them, and the tones connected to chest voice.

Most of the tones of all female singers' lower range, from C2 downward, can be easily produced with an *incorrect union* of both registers; one that was not achieved by starting the tone with the *detached falsetto*. The nature of the *detached* falsetto often eludes many female singers. For them, the solution to finding the detached falsetto, especially in the lower range, is by apply many applications of the tiny u (oo) vowel with the tones located above C2. These *Middle* and *Top Range's* tones are extremely tiny and *"small spaced"*, throat-wise. Their relationship to the *"solid"* quality of the chest voice often seems remote to most female singers, but by applying the u (oo) vowel in the *Middle* and *Top Ranges*, with the softest dynamic possible, and a full flow of breath, it will help to distinguish, by contrast, the ethereal, airy, detached falsetto, from the solidity of the chest voice .

These advanced falsetto tones, with their accompanying *"puffy throat sensations"*, are more readily available *after* the singer has sung for a while, with the "connected mode" of the singing voice, and then attempts to bring the voice into the "detached mode". This so because, afterward singing for a period of time in the *connect mode*, there will remain, with the detached head voice tones, a tiny bit of lingering solidity of the chest voice, which is an indication of how the *detached voice* eventually becomes more "solid". In that way, the progressive growth of the falsetto voice can be monitored. These new versions of the detached falsetto voice must then become, from that point forward, the model for the detached falsetto starting-tone.

Protecting the Singing Voice after it has been completely structure

Once the antagonistic forces of the two registers have been trained to respond to each other in a harmonious team effort, they still remain forever vulnerable to misuse and abuse. Therefore, the structured vocal range must be continually protected, and preserved in its ideal state. The most vulnerable section of the complete range is *the true, lower registers' break area*, located between *middle C* and the *E♮ above it*, plus the "upper registers' break"—C2 to E2. Here are some rules that will help the singer to protect these highly vulnerable tones, as well as the rest of her range.

1) The *"mixed voice"* is responsible for the greater percentage of the *"work element"* with all the tones of the singing voice, *but in particular*, the *tones of the registers' break area.* With the passing of time and correct use, these tones grow in strength and become capable of producing a great deal of volume, used for "dramatic" singing. However, it is to the singer's advantage to sing more *"lyrically"* than "dramatically" during the earlier years of her career. *"Lyric"* singing requires a more restrained use of volume than does "dramatic singing". When *"dramatic singing"* is called for, the singer must test the safety of her singing by observing, after having applied *"dramatic"* volume, to learn if each of the registers' break tones can still be reduced in volume to a *ppp* dynamic. It is also advisable for the singer to periodically review all the rules which originally brought the tones of both the *"upper"* and *"lower"* registers' break areas to their state of correct harmony and function.

2) All the tones of both the *upper* and *lower* registers' break areas must be permanently tuned or *"tilted"* upward, toward the *Top Range.* The quality and muscular actions of these tones must be permanently "matched" to the advanced developed, falsetto voice. The dominant muscular controls of the *"mixed voice"* must be brought downward in the range, during each warm-up sessions, and made to overlap *all the tones of the chest voice.*

3) All ascending scales and vocal phrases must be executed in a guarded manner which incorporates the muscular help of the *mixed voice,* which must forever subjugate and dominate the negative tendencies of the chest voice. This is necessary because, the chest voice is forever ready to break loose from the muscular controls of the mixed voice *(especially when performing ascending scales and vocal phrases),* and cause damage *to the "curved", vertically ascending pathway of the resonance channel.*

4) The critical crossing tones of the true, lower registers' break, E♮ and F♮ above middle C, and the E♮2 and F♮2 natural above C2—the *"upper registers' break"*—must be matched in quality and strength to the qualities and actions of the *advanced developed falsetto*, in order for the singer to maintain a smooth transition from one register to the other. These four above tones, in both lower and upper locations, must be forever sung with their "hookup points" positioned *upward*, toward the upper register's muscular controls, *rather than downward* toward the lower register's muscular controls. Maintaining this important upward focus will help the singer to avoid a deterioration of the divisional "crossover" point, between the two registers. Should any deterioration occur, it could accelerate and cause the two registers to break apart and divide the complete range. From that point on, the inherent antagonism, which each register originally held for the other, will return and deny the singer her superior singing.

In closing

I wish each and every one of my readers success in attaining a superior vocal instrument. The journey toward that goal is long and hard, but—have faith, and never stop trying.

Anthony Frisell

෨෩

Is there an "American School" of classic voice training?
If so—has it failed American singers?

Hundreds of years after the creation of Grand Opera by the Italians—beginning with an early era of virtuoso singers such as *Pistocchi, Senesino, Carestini, Farinelli, Guadagni,* then broad-jumping forward to more familiar names, *Maurel, Tamagno, De Reszke, Nordica, Melba, Sembrich, Eames, Calvé, Shumann-Heink,* then arriving at the afterglow of a more recent *"golden age of song,"* we had such artists as *Ruffo, Tetrazzini, Galli-Curci, Caruso, Ponselle, Gigli, Lauri-Volpi, Pinza, Rethberg, Tibett, Flagstad, Melchior,* then taking another broad jump in time, we enjoyed the glorious singing *of Bjöerling, Warren, Simionato, Stevens, Milanov, Tebaldi, Tucker, Merill, Peerce, Del Monaco, Treigle, London, Sutherland, Pavarotti, Horne. Caballé* to mention but a few—finally we arrive at 2006 and have to concede that presently, it is almost unanimously acknowledged that there are no singers trained by the "American School" capable of successfully singing the main-stream repertory of Italian Grand Opera, especially the operas of Verdi and Puccini.

After retiring, many famous singers from the above great periods created their own vocal teaching studios and passed down the superior vocal training methods of the old "Italian School," which they themselves had learned. Some of them came to America and taught many outstanding American singers. Then, about the end of the *50s* in America, the traditions of the *"old Italian School"* vanished. Was this due to a communication break between the voice teachers of the past and those of the present? Or a revolutionary attitude of arrogance and superiority on the part of a new breed of American voice teachers who emerged after the Second World War? Long after this critical *disconnect* had occurred, echoes of the old Italian School's teaching terms and applications still lingered about in many American voice training studios. The "new" teachers were superficially aware of such "old school" principles as *vocal registers, resonance cavities, positions and movements of the tongue and soft palate, low breathing* and *diaphragmatic support.* And some of them bantered them about, to establish their own authority. But they simply didn't believe in their validity and worth, so they swiftly went about creating a new approach to voice training which they believed was "simpler" and "faster." The new school of teachers eventually came to believe that the only sources of the singing voice are the larynx and the vocal cords and that the contributions of the so-called *registers,* the various *resonance cavities,* and the *positions and movements of the tongue and soft palate* were of no importance.

After so many years have passed, we *can't* say for sure that those post World War II teachers did indeed create a new "American School" of voice training. However, when so many American singers auditioning for roles of the mainstream Italian operatic repertory fail technically to qualify to sing them and consistently present similar vocal flaws and mannerisms, we must assume that they were all trained in a manner using similar based principles.

The manner in which the "new school" transformed their teaching principles and practices *away from the old Italian Schoo*l was to immediately do away with five of the old School's major principles:

1. There exist two distinct and separate vocal registers within the complete range of tones of all singers, male and female, of all vocal categories and more importantly, these two registers are inherently antagonistic toward each other. In order to "produce" a successful singer, these two registers' muscular actions and vocal sounds must be made musically and muscularly compatible.

2. A critically important section of all singers' complete range, known as the *passaggio*—the tones between B♭ below middle C to the G♮ above it—functions radically differently from all other tones of the complete range, and while singing them, the breath's "motor force," necessary to evoke and control these *passaggio* tones, has to be applied in a "different manner" than when singing anywhere else in the range.

    3. The singer's *tongue* and *soft palate* play critically important roles with the *passaggio* tones, and their positions and movements determine the success or failure of the singer to control the passaggio tones. For example, when the tongue's position is correct, it rises upward and out of the lower throat channel and into the mouth-pharynx cavity, where it arches and imitates the shape of the hard palate, situated just above it. The *soft palate, which serves as a damper,* allows the singer to properly regulate the amount of air flow of the tones from B♭ below middle C, upward to the top of the range and must be made to position itself forward and downward—*not upward*—as is generally and erroneously believed.

    4. With every individual tone of the singer's complete range, there exist progressive, muscular adjustments required of the singer in order to accomplish the tone's total fulfillment. These adjustments are implemented as follows:

    A) The singer starts a tone which is controlled by the "detached falsetto" voice, and which, if properly evoked, only evokes the *first layer* of vocal cords' participation of the selected tone. This means that the tone is *without* any of the vocal cords' vibrato action.

    B) The singer then further intensifies the breath force, and that calls into play the *second layer* of the vocal cords' participation, once known as the "mixed voice," wherein tiny, puffy pulses of the vocal cords' vibratory actions are added to the "starter tone."

    C) Finally, the fullest force of breath pressure is added to the tone, and that adds a *third, final layer* of the vocal cords' vibratory action to the tone, which brings the tone to total fulfillment, a condition known technically as the "connected voice, or the performing voice." The terms "detached," "mixed voice" and "full" or "performing voice" were standard teaching, directional terms of the old

    Italian School, and some of them are still used today by a few voice teachers but without them having the same meaning as in the past. This is so because the new school of teaching did away with the critically important detached falsetto voice, which is the first layer of vocal cords' participation with any tone; which, when further developed, creates the "mixed voice," or second layer of vocal cords' participation, leading to the development of the "third layer of the vocal cords' participation" or the "full voice" or "performing voice".

    5. The classic Italian vowels, as pronounced and modified by native Italians, play a major role in correctly accomplishing the above critical factors of superior vocal structuring and singing, and no other language, other than Italian, accomplishes the same superior results. The *passaggio* tones are the most difficult to understand and even more difficult for the singer to solve their physiological, structural needs. These needs can only be structured and properly "placed" into the singer's complete range by strengthening the muscles of the *head voice* register. Briefly stated, this is accomplished by evoking the muscular controls of the top range's tones while *avoiding all contact with chest voice power,* then slowly imposing the *head voice's* muscular controls upon all the tones of the singer's complete range by carrying those

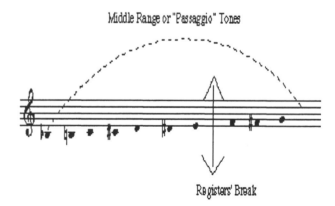

Middle Range or "Passaggio" Tones

Registers' Break

controls downward, tone by tone, from the top range downward to the lowest note of the *chest voice*.

The aw vowel, which has completely vanished from present-day teaching, is the best for accomplishing the above. The aw is a combination of the *u (oo), o (oh) and a (ah) vowels,* and it is better than all of the five other vowels, u (oo), i (ee), e (eh), o (oh) and a (ah), because it allows for the greatest, free flow of the breath stream, which is the *motor power* that generates all vocal tones.

Male singers should note that the tones shown in the illustration above represent the *upper middle range* of their voices, while these same tones represent the bottom of *all female singers'* range.

The tedious process of completely resolving the problems of the *passaggio's* tones takes a very long time to accomplish, perhaps *four or five years,* when one knows the proper exercises. In some cases, where the "raw" chest register's power has been forced upward in the range to its top limit at E♮ above middle C, it takes longer, since *the wrong chest voice power* must first be "undone." This is accomplished by applying *seemingly endless,* descending, *detached falsetto scales* to them, with the falsetto form of the u (oo) and i (ee) vowels, then gradually imposing the strengthened head voice muscles' control upon all the tones of the chest voice. The *passaggio's* tones *do not exist* as a separate, muscular, harmonic group until they have been transformed *away from their original state,* into a new arrangement wherein some of their *muscular controls* are drawn from the bottom range and others from the top range. It is comforting to know that structuring the *passaggio's* tones has always been confusing and problematic since the very beginning of man's attempts to understand the nature of and train the singing voice hundreds of years ago. During all past, great periods of vocal training, an experienced teacher knew, from the outset of vocal training, that he/she must never "drive" the power of the chest voice upward in the range as far as the E♮ above middle C. By doing so, it will deny the student the possibility of "making harmonic" the inherent antagonism that exists between the two registers—especially between B♭ below middle C to the G♮ natural situated above it—which is the only way the singer will ever possess a full, smooth and even, complete range of tones from bottom to top.

In direct opposition to the above principle, the new school's dictum was—*do indeed extend the chest register's range upward past middle C to the E♮ above it*! This was not only incorrect, but it was blatantly contrary to historical pedagogic practices. For example, Manuel Garcia's table of registration events demonstrates a considerable overlap between the *chest* and *head* registers. All correctly structured tones of the *passaggio* are a creation of *mind, determination, specific knowledge and will,* and lots of time. The superior singing voice *is not* created from the speaking voice, nor is it an extension of it. It is slowly created from an *entirely different set of muscles,* the *head voice group.* The singing voice's muscles are located far above the speaking voice's range. They are frequently referred to as the *falsetto voice for all males* and the *flute voice* or *whistle voice for all females.* The purest form and applications of these muscles *(free from any and all chest voice)* can only be accessed from the *very top range* of every singer's voice where they perpetually allow the fullest, free-flow of the breath stream. Great skill is necessary in arranging the throat position of the presently sung vowel of any tone, high upward, in the posterior area of the mouth-pharynx cavity, behind the soft and hard palates, which is necessary to enable a full, strong flow of breath, speeding upward from the bottom of the resonance tract, to reach these tones and grant the singer absolute muscular control of them. At the beginning of training, these "hollow," "breathy" *falsetto* or *whistle-voice, top-range-tones,* convey very little of their true worth, nor what finally emerges at advanced levels of training.

The Soprano Voice—131

William Shakespeare, the famous singer and one of *Lamperti, perè's* best vocal students *(not the famous English playwright)*, stated the following in his masterfully written vocal manual *The Art of Singing (Oliver Ditson Company)*: "If, while singing a high note, as softly as possible, *(a detached falsetto tone; author's note)*, and the note is accompanied by a sensation of sound and a full flow of the breath stream reverberating and ringing towards the back of the head, *beyond the last upper teeth*, we shall have discovered the so-called head voice."

Throughout the international singing community, past and present, the *five classic Italian vowels, u (oo), i (ee), e (eh), o (oh), and a (ah),* as pronounced by native Italians, have been considered best for training the singing instrument. This is so because the Italian language is essentially free from diphthongs; whereas the most disadvantageous language for training the singing voice is English, as it is presently spoken by native Americans, since it abounds in diphthongs. A pure vowel allows for a specific, single throat position for any selected tone. To the contrary, a tone that employs a diphthong, which toggles between one of its vowels to its other, *does not quickly* "settle down" in the throat to allow the singer to establish a single, specific vowel throat position. This is because the diphthong-factor, being imposed upon a selected tone, confuses the singer as to which of the diphthong's two vowels should be made the dominant vowel of the two, in order to steady the tone's proper throat position *so that pitch accuracy and vowel purity can be resolved.*

A frequently overlooked factor about the classic Italian vowels is that, when they are being taught to English speaking students, they are invariably *filtered* through the sieve of the teacher's American pronunciation of them. Doing this unavoidably alters and misshapen the pure Italian vowels away from their original pure forms, thereby denying the student their Italian benefits. Not only is there a vast difference in the basic sound of each "misshapen" Italian vowel, wrongly pronounced in a flat, dull, strident manner, but there are also vast physical movements of the tongue, lips, and cheeks that accompany the *proper* production of each of the five classic Italian vowels. And, most American *repertory coaches* are also filtering the Italian language through the English language when they endeavor to "correct a student's Italian pronunciation." When that be the case, it stands to reason that the Italian vowels are no longer remotely able to help the singer correctly perform the various vocal exercises necessary to build a superior singing voice, nor to create the same superior "tonal sounds" that result, as when the Italian vowels are being properly produced. It will prove most beneficial for all vocal students if they will apply the classic Italian vowels to their singing voices, exclusively, for at least the *first seven years* of their training.

Here's what *William Shakespeare* had to say about the movements of the *lips, tongue and facial muscles:* While singing: "The command over the expression of the eyes depends upon the freedom of action of the muscles around them; but as these muscles work in sympathy with the muscles which control the face, and which raise the upper lip *(while the vowel being sung properly places the tongue and palate)*, all will act free, *if the face is free,* and all will act rigidly, *if the face is rigid.*"

The detached falsetto versions of the i (ee) and e (eh) vowels help the singer to understand the "lift up" principle. The "lift up" involves certain movements of the lips, cheeks and tongue which elevate the entire upper section of the range (for all singers) away from the entire bottom section of the range, starting at Cs above middle C upward, for all male singers, and Cs2 and upward, for all female singers, to the very top of the range.

Accomplishing the "lift up" while exercising the voice or while singing enables the singer to maintain muscular harmony and balance between the upper *dominant area* of the complete vocal range and the lower *subordinate area* of the complete range by subordinating, as the singer ascends the range, all negative aspects of the lower range, such as inappropriate bulk and weight, upon arriving at the critical C♯ for male singers, and C♯2 for all female singers. The "lift up" principle is a very important factor for achieving superior singing. Present-day training principles do not consider the "lift up" but oppose its critically important principles by applying exercises that create a rigid jaw and restrictive movements of the lips, cheeks, and tongue. These inappropriate vocal exercises quickly and undeniably create a permanent antagonism between the upper and lower areas of the singer's complete range. This forces all singers, whose training *excludes* the important "lift up" principle, to almost totally negate the bottom area from their complete range.

When advanced American vocal students begin to audition for their first operatic roles, they are frequently required to present several vocal selections *in various foreign languages*, usually Italian, French, German, Russian, and sometimes English. Nothing shows more *ignorance,* on the part of those individuals holding these auditions, of the true nature of a superior singing instrument, nor its structural requirements, where "language-influence" is concerned. By them requiring this damaging audition-policy, it also shows a lack of consideration for the singers' voices.

Italian operas were composed in Italian, to be sung by Italian speaking singers—essentially, *all Italian operas are dramatic.* These Italian opera composers sought out "dramatic" stories that presented them with a full range of human experiences: sorrow, joy, happiness, success, tragedy, betrayal, and almost always, in the end, they ended with death. The music which these Italians composed for these dramatic operas had to fulfill the high peaks and low valleys of human emotions. These dramatic operas required exceptional singers who can sing with a full range of dynamics and a large variety of vocal timbres: sad, happy, angry, surprised, joyful, betrayed, disappointed, passionate and loving. Those singers who could bring the Italian composer's scores to life possessed superior vocal techniques. To make a point, how could any soprano, when singing Puccini's Tosca, in the second act, after Tosca has murdered Scarpia, fulfill the dramatic moment that Puccini intended *if she does not* possess a *mixed chest register* for Tosca's declamation: *"E avanti a lui tremava tutta Roma!"*, like the thrilling *mixed chest voice* of *Zinka Milanov, Claudia Muzio,* or *Renata Tebaldi*?

Surely you have your own favorite moment in one of the great Italian operas, when a certain famous singer sang a phrase in a particular manner that thrilled you to the core of your being and which no other singer thereafter ever accomplished for you in the same way. All superior Italian singers of the past, and some more recently, could sing a full range of tones, all of which possessed brilliance in their centers and velvety roundness around their center; what the early Italian teachers called *chiaroscuro,* "brightness and darkness" combined. A tone with a bright, diamond center with a rim of darkness surrounding it could be sung very softly and sweetly, when that was appropriate, then loudly and "blaring" when that was necessary—tones which were called *squillo,* meaning tones that "blared out" like a trumpet without either extreme of dynamic, loud and/or soft being threatened or eliminated by the other.

It should be noted that, during the student's early period of training, where applications of the five, classic Italian vowels are concerned, there exists a potential for students to produce overly bright or "shrill" tones. Manuel Garcia addressed this issue in his 1840 Paris manual, *Hints on Singing.* He advised one of his pupils *". . . don't be concerned about shrillness of tone in the beginning of training, for it is easily converted away from shrillness, by rounding the vowels."* Meaning that, a voice need not be polished until it arrives at an advanced stage of development. "Rounding the voice" evolves certain exercises that utilize the u (oo), o (oh), and aw vowels.

The best American singers, of the past forty years or more, often achieved a certain "roundness" with many of their tones, but in most cases, these tones still lacked brilliance, especially in the bottom range, with *female singers* and in the top range with *male singers*. The cause of this *"timbre-deficient imbalance"* can be traced to the fact that the new school teachers lacked the knowledge as to how to correctly structure the *passaggio*, or passageway's, tones. The dictionary defines a passageway as *a corridor; a narrow track of space, forming a hallway, through which an individual may transit through, in either direction; or a path through which an object, a chair or piano, or what have you, may be transported through.*

If the singer will envision the *passaggio* as being *a narrow corridor* that connects one part of the range to another and which the singer is obliged to send the breath stream into and then through, *in both ascending and descending directions*, the singer will have established a clear cut image of the passaggio. Then the singer may proceed to the problems which cause such difficulties with the *passaggio's* tones.

Rather than to go into all the numerous details necessary to do this *(they can be easily had by reading my manual A Singer's Notebook)*, it will prove quicker and more enlightening to explain the two major differences between a singer who possesses a superiorly structured *passaggio and one who possesses a poorly, incompletely structured passaggio.*

Scenario # 1: When a singer possesses a properly structured *passaggio,* he/she can easily sing all its tones with superior tonal quality, pure vowels, and control of all ranges of dynamics *because there are no obstacles along the pathway of the complete passaggio which block the air flow.* The following facts are critically important. Other than negative effects upon the vocal organs due to illness, which may cause infection and consequential swelling of the vocal organs the two main "blockers" of the passaggio tones' proper function are: *the incorrect positions and movements of the tongue and the soft palate.*

When the tongue and soft palate's movements and positions are correct, they grant the singer free entry for the energized breath stream *(which is the generator of all the passaggio's tones)* into each and every tone of the *passaggio*, then further upward, along the resonance tract, *to the very top notes of the range.* To the beginner, desperately trying to solve the problems of his/her *passaggio,* this may seem naive and too simple and radical an explanation of the *passaggio's* main problems,, but to any advanced singer, these tongue and soft palate factors represent indisputable truth.

Scenario #2: Conversely, when the singer is denied a facile entry into his/her *passaggio tones* (which negatively affect his/her top tones), and is told that the problems of his/her *passaggio* are the incorrect movements and positioning of his/her tongue and soft palate, he/she seldom believes these factors and instead places the blame on other remote, unrealistic and non-related factors for the "blockage" they experience with their passaggio tones.

The critical structural needs of the *passaggio* of most American *male* singers—tenors, baritones, and basses—are generally unknown, *and are seldom properly addressed*, while the student changes from one voice teacher to another in a futile attempt to gain a functional singing voice. No teacher seems to offer them any alternatives to their problems, other than vocal compromises such as: "covering the tone" [a method of holding off the chest voice's brilliance which dulls down the tone(s), and/or *"shrinking the volume of the tone(s)],"* "humming before singing," *"vocalizing with one particular vowel, exclusively,"* or the most damaging of all, by merely "shouting" the passaggio tones with the promise that they will eventually become musically polished, highly controllable tones.

You may personally experience and thereby understand some of these above negative factors, by going to the back of the auditorium *when the male singers are singing* and focusing your attention upon the variety of inaccurate, unmusical vocal maneuvers and unpleasant tonal timbres which repeatedly occur, with certain tones, along the path of the singer's complete range. The singer's vocal timbres will vary from "dark," "dull," "inaudible," "inferior," "radically open," or "restrictively closed," with severe distortions of the five singing vowels and, in some areas of the range, a few "bright," "clear," "projecting" tones that "hint of professional possibilities, but in general, the singer's efforts present a far-below-standard condition with little promise.

Unfailingly, the male singer's bottom range is barely audible, and most of his tones possess a covered, "smothered" quality. The voice sounds "tired" and "worn." As the singer ascends toward his middle range, the voice grows uncontrollably louder but not better in quality. Control over the dynamics produces "coarse, unmusical shouting." Some lyric tenors avoid these undesirable factors by almost completely negating the brilliance of the chest voice's vibrato with all their tones, from Fn above middle C *downward to the very bottom of their range,* and by singing excessively softly and sweetly with a soprano-like quality. The Italians derogatorily call these singers *"tenorinos."* They appear to successfully sing the *"bel canto"* lyric repertory for a brief period of time then suddenly vanish, suggesting that something was missing from their voices from the start. Indeed, it was the full collaboration of the chest voice with their exaggeratedly developed head voice muscles!

Every serious singer who places high hopes on someday enjoying a successful, professional singing career should make this infallible, highly revelatory test of his/her voice. Make a recording of one of your best sung arias, one that you feel best demonstrates and justifies why you should be hired by a major operatic theater manager to sing an operatic role for a two or three-thousand member audience of opera lovers. Then make a second recording, placing your best sung vocal selection next to *(either before or after)* a recording of one of great singers of the past, singing the same vocal selection as your own. Listen carefully to it over and over before reaching your conclusions. Admittedly, doing this would be frightening, maybe devastating, but it will definitely inform you of your true worth as a singer. During a live performance of an operatic role, if you've "really got it", the audience will burst into enthusiastic applause. If you *don't* have it, they'll applaud politely and sparingly. In some Italian cities, when a singer falls short of the audience's standards, they are "booed" off the stage! Go ahead, find the courage to be your own critically judging audience! This is practically the only occasion when I would recommend to a singer to make a recording of his/her voice, since I believe that doing so, during the long period of training necessary to acquire a great singing technique, is counterproductive.

As far as the purity of the five Italian classic vowels and the manner in which they effect the basic sound of most American male singers' voices are concerned, American singers generally sound *less like the great Italian singers of the past* than do female American singers. This is because, almost unfailingly, most American male singers rely almost exclusively on the speaking voice's vowel sounds and muscular controls to structure their bottom notes, which are the easiest notes of their complete ranges, and to accomplish these "forgeries." For more than five decades now, this mistaken concept—"model your singing voice on your speaking voice"—has *lured* the average American student into falsely believing that the above approach is the only solution to attaining a superior singing voice.

Admittedly, it is much more difficult for *a male student* to achieve a superior singing voice than for a female student. This is because the male singer's total range of tones possess more *chest voice tones* than *head voice tones*, through which most vocal problems find their solutions. Most American male singers' voices lack brilliance and are "hollow" and "foggy" sounding. They sound like an "older singer," who has been singing "heavy repertory" for far too long, even when the singer is young and at the beginning of his training. There also exists a tragically erroneous concept that the singing voices of all singers, as they grow older, thickens and darkens in sound. Huh! That's only the case when the technique is incorrect.

When *Garcia perè,* during his later years, came to America to sing the role of *the barber*, in Rossini's *Il Barbiere di Siviglia,* the American impresario who had hired Garcia, along with his talented children, because of their "world famous name," knowing well it would draw crowds, was astounded upon first hearing that the "old man's voice" had retained the youthful freshness and beauty of tone of a superior singer, which indeed Garcia was. After completing an extensive tour of many major American cities, Garcia perè and his talented kids returned to Europe, smiling with satisfaction and with their pockets full of American dollars.

Most American female singers structure their voices in quite the opposite way than do their American male counterparts. They generally focus their attention on their top octave's tones and neglect their bottom octave's tones. This is so because all female singers' "true" *passaggio* is located at the bottom of their range, which is so difficult to understand and "fix" and which can be *temporarily* ignored. Even when a female singer can sing with reasonably good sounding tones at the upper middle and top of her range and convinces herself that she has "escaped" all the negative influences of her chest register's "unattractive" and "unladylike," difficult-to-control tones, in reality she has made the same fatal mistake that most American male singers have made *when they neglected the use of their head voice's falsetto tones. Most female singers hold a belief that their voices possess "two passaggios," an upper and lower.* That's OK. *That theory has been treated in great detail, in my vocal manual, A Singer's Notebook.*

Going once again to the back of the auditorium and *listening to a female singer sing,* one immediately observes that their bottom range is weak and almost inaudible, but as the singer ascends toward her *upper middle range,* the basic quality and "pronunciation" of her vowels improve. Then suddenly, the top range "blooms," and the singer takes advantage of her best-of-all singing tones. However, these top tones never possess the true brilliance of *"squillo"* tones, *which blare out over the orchestra and into the audience.* Unfortunately, the early promise of a future successful career eventually wanes, and the voice suddenly and unexplainably fails.

Most American female singers generally sound as if they are singing in some foreign language. However, upon closer scrutiny, one realizes they are attempting to sing in English but instead produce some otherworldly form of Italian or French with a "choked throat" in the lower octave of their range. Once again, a neglected, under-developed *passaggio* is the culprit causing these gross and inhibiting vocal limitations.

The absence of brilliance of most of the American female singers' lower range is caused by the tongue and soft palate's faulty positions and movements; both act like bathtub plugs at the lower and upper entrances to the *true "bottom" passaggio*—at B♭ below middle C up to the G♮ above it—and block the motor force of the breath stream from surging upward from the lungs into the *passaggio,* then further upward in the range toward the middle and top ranges. Once these "plugs" have been removed *(this takes quite a long time),* the *passaggio's tones* and all the remaining top tones of the complete range will gain the much needed, but formerly missing, vocal timbres of brilliance and grant the singer complete control of the breath dynamics and correct formations of the five classic Italian vowels. At their best, most American female singers sound forever juvenile. They seldom achieve the "full," "round," "warm," "womanly" vocal timbres and dynamics necessary to sing the great heroines of the mainstream, dramatic, Italian, operatic repertory.

For nearly forty-five years now, since right after the Second World War, most American singers *have never been presented with the proper methods of utilizing the motor force of breath. That's why* so many American singers, male and female, present little or no timbre variations with their singing and instead sing in a dull, monochromatic, juvenile fashion.

The inherent but wrong pathway of the breath stream, when English is the singer's primary language, directs the breath stream into the mouth-pharynx cavity, then forward toward the lower front teeth; then it exits the mouth cavity, accomplishing none of what is necessary to sing superior tones. The *correct pathway* is backward and upward, in the mouth-pharynx cavity, then behind both the hard and soft palates, and into either the resonance cavities of the sinuses or those of the skull. *All the above is the reason why most American voice students are consistent users of the incorrect and unproductive shallow breathing method*, as opposed to employing *correct,* "low, diaphragmatic breathing."

Admittedly, English-speaking students cannot quickly nor easily *reroute* their "breath stream" onto the correct pathway. This is because the muscular patterns of their tongue, lips, and cheeks, while attempting to sing, *do not* operate in the same manner as when the five classic Italian vowels are operating correctly. *A major talent of all superior singers* is their skill in directing the breath stream into a specific resonance cavity where the assigned pitch is located. This skill can only be perfected when each of the five classical Italian vowels is being properly sung. Each correctly sung Italian vowel positions the upper posterior area of the mouth-pharynx cavity in a precise manner, one which enables the breath stream to flow freely into the desired resonance cavity, appropriate to the assigned pitch; upon arriving within the appropriate resonance cavity, the tone's quality is automatically enhanced and its volume amplified due to the size and shape of the resonance cavity itself, all of which produces a superior tone.

After the singer takes in an exaggerated amount of breath, holds it back, momentarily, within the lungs *(a factor which builds up breath pressure necessary to create a motor force)*, then "gradually *releases the breath stream,"* allowing it to whiz toward the vocal cords where it passes through the glottis *(the opening between the vocal cords, the only "door" into and out of the lungs)*, then, at that point, the singer must adjust his/her tongue, lips and cheeks in order to adjust the posterior throat position of the assigned vowel and in order to succeed in directing the breath stream into the appropriate resonance cavity. Managing the proper "pronunciation" of the selected Italian vowel *(something radically different than when speaking)* greatly helps the singer to accomplish this task in a smooth and musical manner, employing superior *mental imagery* in an indirect and somewhat unconscious manner.

If all the above *is not* properly accomplished, there is still a possibility of the *inferior* singer producing the intended pitch(es) with a reasonably pure vowel and an acceptable quality; however, *without the fullest potential amount of the breath flow having been properly directed into the appropriate resonance cavity* and then *"focusing the tone"* into the center of the cavity, or the "bull's eye," the effort results in inferior tone. In the old days, the "bull's eye" was called the *point d'apui* by the French and the *punto d'appogiare* by the Italians. Setting up this "bull's eye", in its precise place, within any of the resonance cavities, towards which the singer must aim the breath stream, is accomplished by applying various structural exercises using the *head voice's i (ee)* vowel.

The above situation describes the *best* of what could occur when the breath stream is correctly managed; conversely, the *worst* results *will definitely occur* when the breath stream is *improperly* managed. When that happens, the singer, *despite good intentions,* is obliged to "reach away" from the proper controls of the breath stream and instead "grab hold" of the wrong sets of muscles, which produces *"forced resonance,"* as the old Italian teachers described it. Doing so causes the lower jaw to stiffen and *evokes the negative power of the chest voice's muscular control*s which, immediately causes rigidity of all the *passaggio's* tones, resulting in inferior tonal qualities, compromised vowels, and faulty intonations.

Each correctly produced Italian vowel exerts a strong, individual, positive muscular influence on any and all tones of the singer's complete range. The *u (oo), o (oh)* and *a (ah)* vowels group themselves together, and they perform as the "open throat" vowels but to varying degrees of openness. This means that the open or closed manner in which the vowels position the upper posterior area of the throat is progressive. Starting from a *partially open throat position* with the u (oo) vowel, then moving toward a slightly more open throat position with the o (oh) vowel, then finally with the bright, fully open a (ah) vowel, the singer arrives at a fully open throat position.

The *first group* of vowels, *u (oo), o (oh) and a (ah)*, enables the singer to emit and properly direct the maximum flow of the breath, critically essential to producing all superior tone. Especially useful is the <u>aw</u> vowel which is a combination of the *u (oo), o (oh)* and *a (ah)*. These three vowels, plus the <u>aw</u>, are very congenial for producing the maximum amount of breath flow. They help the singer generate free, open-throated, round, vibrant, consistently available tones. However, neither the *u (oo), o (oh)*, nor the *a (ah)* vowels grant the singer *tonal brilliance, vocal focus,* or *precise vocal placement.* Those precious attributes are only acquired through the use of the *head voice versions* of the *i (ee)* and *e (eh)* vowels. In any case, the superior singer, who possesses a near-perfectly structured singing voice, *can sing all five vowels easily and purely* on any and all of the tones of his/her complete range.

The training procedures of the average American student usually rely upon the *u (oo)* and *o (oh)* vowels and a dark, compromised, "covered" *a (ah)* vowel. There are but few who rely upon the *i (ee)* and *e (eh)* vowels to keep their voices going because, very quickly, the initial help of the *incorrect* i (ee) and e (eh) vowels run out of their "tricks." This is because these singers are *employing a wrong version of the i (ee) and e (eh) vowels,* one based exclusively upon *chest register muscular dominance.* Correct and "safe" versions of the *i (ee) and e (eh) vowels* are *the head voice versions of them,* which must be used exclusively to build the voice. Much later, the advanced *head voice* versions of the i (ee) and e (eh) vowels will reveal to the singer the correct manner of singing the i (ee) and e (eh) vowels in the bottom range of the voice by ways of "reflection" and "imitation" of the head voice's muscular actions and tonal timbres.

Generally speaking, the first group of vowels—the *u (oo), o (oh) a (ah)*—produces readily accessible "breathy," "hollow" voices, which *lack* tonal "brilliance" and precise focus, meaning that the tone is not properly directed toward its *center-of-the-bull's-eye* throat position, especially with the singer's top tones. If a singing teacher is aware that the *u (oo), o (oh) and a (ah) vowels* are permanently antagonistic to the *i (ee) and e (eh) vowels* and that each individual group is capable of achieving certain important structural accomplishments, which the other group *can not* accomplish, then he/she is a rare teacher, indeed.

Few students accept the stinging reality that most great singers of the past took *many years* to build their voices to perfection. *Giovanni Sbriglia (1832-1916)* one of the old Italian School's greatest singer/teachers, stated that it took him *nine years* to convert *Jean de Reszke's (1850-1925)* voice from an unsuccessful baritone into one of the greatest tenors of all times. *Emma Calvé (1858-1942),* who *Mathilde Marchesi (1821-1913)* trained to become one of the brightest stars of the Paris Opera, decided that her vocal technique limited her to lyric roles, while she longed to sing the "gutsy" dramatic roles in opera. So ambitious *Calvé* started searching for a teacher who could correctly build her *chest tones, but none was found.* Luckily, she eventually found the great *castrato Dommenico Mustafà* who accomplished her wishes. Mustafà taught her the secrets of correctly structuring her *chest tones* through the use of the *voix mixte (a combination of head voice and chest voice muscular "blendings," applied with an exaggerated breath flow, and certain, little-known vocal exercises, which had granted Mustafà his own great singing voice).* *Calvé* described *Mustafà's mixed chest tone*s as *"certain curious notes...strange, sexless, superhuman, uncanny!"*

A great voice teacher, besides possessing a seemingly endless store of technical knowledge about voice building, plus great skills in applying that knowledge, must also possess superior hearing skills since without them, he/she could not make critical judgments and decisions as to what each individual voice lacks or already possesses and how to go about granting his/her students all their voice's positive needs, while eliminating all their faults.

F. Husler, the famous German voice teacher of *Leoni Ryseneck, Sàndor Kónya,* and soprano *Karen Bransen,* all of the Metropolitan Opera, had much to say about the teacher's hearing: *"We no longer have at our disposal the acute sense of hearing once possessed by great teachers of singing of the past... Our ears have lost that strange kind of intuitive, almost somnambulistic intelligence, together with its extraordinary, accurate, discriminating faculty."*

Sàndor Kónya studied with me for the last seven and a half years of his Metropolitan Opera career, and *Karen Bransen*, also of *"the Met,"* for about two years. *I did not teach Leoni Ryseneck.* I also taught Metropolitan tenor *Flaviano Labó* off and on, for approximately two years. Since he was so successful, he had to frequently leave town for an engagement with one or more of the great opera houses of the world. Of course it must be acknowledged that before working with me, *Mr. Labó* had already studied with several illustrious voice teachers, such as *Gina Cigna, Carmen Melis, Apollo Grandforte, and Ettore Campogallilani.*

But voice training *is not* a solo act—it is a collaboration, and each superior teacher requires a superior student in order to produce a great singer. *But where is such a rare creature during these unusual, troubled, financially strained times?* Most present-day students are ill-prepared for the long, testy course of vocal training that a superior teacher would lay out before him/her, especially when the amount of time needed to complete it varies from individual to individual and is unpredictable at the start of training.

In closing, and in fairness to the dismal picture that I've presented about the so-called "New American School of Voice Training," I'd like to add that presently, in Italy, Italian voice teachers *are not* doing much better than American voice teachers with their production of great "Italian voices" as in the past. Most of their professional singers sing with strident tones that lack "roundness" and "beauty," resulting from one of the *possible negative influences of the Italian language, which is prone to extreme "openness" if not modified by "rounding."*

It is not surprising that most young, hopeful European and Asian voice students are flocking to America for their voice training. However, they are unfortunately basing their decision to come here upon the "canned" singing they've heard on popular American CDs where often the singers' voices have been enhanced by advanced audio techniques, to give them whatever they lack, but all of which would be immediately revealed and recognized if the same singers were heard performing "live" in any major theater.

During the long, testy, tedious process of obtaining a superior singing voice, the "organs" of the singing voice are being transformed away from their inherent behavior, toward new muscular patterns and responses appropriate for the singer to sing demanding vocal music, which is as much an athletic feat as a mental and esthetic one. At the very end of training when the superior singing voice has finally been obtained, and while singing, the vocal organs behave radically different than they once did at the start of training. They *must not* be made to return to serving the old speaking voice! Doing so would throw them out of harmonious balance with each other. It is for that reason that great singers usually adopt a rigid, permanent policy of *limited, soft volume speaking.*

Most American vocal students greatly resist the transformation of their singing organs away from the muscular patterns of their speaking voices and only feel comfortable when their larynx is incorrectly mired in its lowest, immobile position, whereas the larynx must always be free to adjust to the various positions necessary to satisfy accurate intonation and pure vowels. Frequently, after their voice lessons, and *sometimes during a voice lesson,* American students feel that the arrangements of their vocal organs are strange, uncomfortable, disorienting. Because of this, they mistakenly attempt to return the vocal organs to their old, speaking voice's muscular positions and responses. This is both foolish and counterproductive. The serious singer must acknowledge that they can't have the situation both ways—a speaking voice that is available for hours on end for unimportant, daily chatter—or a great, sensitive, beautiful and guarded singing voice that is capable of bringing one of the great operatic masterpieces to life.

If any of my readers truly believe that the vocal organs of a great, professional singer are aligned and related to each other in the same manner as the speaking voice and that the speaking voices' muscular arrangements are capable of permitting the singer to sing a challenging operatic aria, accompanied by a full orchestra, then he/she is living in *"Lollypop Land"* and has never been anywhere close by a great opera singer while he/she is singing a physically demanding aria. Admittedly, there is much more to vocal training than all the above. If the reader wishes to learn more about my own teaching theories and practices, he/she may read one of my many published vocal manuals. For a start, I suggest *A Singer's Notebook* and *The Art of Singing on the Breath Flow,* which can be purchased through *Patelson's Music House, 160 West 56th Street, in Manhattan, NY. Tel: 212-757-5587.*

Thank you very much for your interest and patience. Always keep in mind that I am a sincere and faithful friend of the singer and very sympathetic to his/her outrageously challenging plight! Therefore, I close with a fantasy-dream about a coming vocal-teaching revolution, followed by a *renaissance* of the great training techniques of classical singing that produce great singers. I'm presently searching for allies to bring that *renaissance* about. So, get serious and do join me in the cause.

With best wises and much affection,

Anthony Frisell April 2006 — New York City

Anthony Frisell

Anthony Frisell was born in New Orleans, Louisiana, of Italian immigrant parents. He first encountered the world of opera through recordings, and would often debate with his boyhood friends about the merits of *Beniamino Gigli* versus *Jussi Bjöerling*. After high school, Frisell studied singing briefly in New York City before returning to New Orleans to take up stage directing with the *New Orleans Opera Company.* There he worked with conductor *Walter Herbert and William Wymetal,* and such great singers as *Richard Tucker, Leonard Warren, Jan Peerce, Dorothy Kirsten, Mario del Monaco, Robert Merrill, Victoria de los Angeles, and Zinka Milanov.*

Mr. Frisell returned to singing for three years under the guidance of *Giovanni Cacetti,* a wealthy opera enthusiast who was the first to introduce Frisell to the "head voice" theories of voice training. Following a brief career as an operatic tenor in Italy, Mr. Frisell returned to New York and developed a school of voice training that resulted in the publication of his first voice book, *The Tenor Voice.* This was followed by *The Soprano Voice* and *The Baritone Voice,* all of which have remained in print and are very popular throughout the world. He has taught many international opera stars.

He was for seven and a half years, the New York teacher of the great tenor *Sándor Kónya,* and for a short time, tenor *Flaviano Labò,* both formerly of the *Metropolitan Opera,* and many other International Opera Houses. And, for several years, baritone *Seymour Swartzman,* formerly of the *New York State Theater.*

Mr. Frisell initially learned about singing from his years as a stage director, working with great operatic singers on stage. While he acknowledges a particular debt to the extraordinary vocal achievements of both *Bjöerling and Milanov,* it is his work with *Milanov* and her remarkable understanding of singing, especially *pianissimo* singing, that has served as his greatest instruction and inspiration.

Mr. Frisell is also an author of fiction; his novels and many of his short stories have been published in Europe. In 1995, *Golden Throat,* his novel about the international world of grand opera, was published in the United States by *Branden Publishing Co. (Brookline Village, Ma.).* Mr. Frisell has recently written the music and libretto for three operas. His first opera *"The Secret of the painting",* is based upon Oscar Wilde's novel—*The Picture Of Dorian Gray.* His second opera *"Rasputin",* is based upon the lives of *Rasputin* and the *Romanovs* of 1917 revolutionary Russia. His third opera, *La Vendetta,* is based upon one of his own, original short stories, of the same name.

Master Classes

given by

Anthony Frisell

Mr. Frisell is available to conduct master classes. He may be contacted in
New York City, at (212) 246-3385